MONEY SAVING
SECRETS
OF SMART
AIRLINE
TRAVELERS

Capt. Richard A. Bodner

BETTERWAY PUBLICATIONS, INC.
White Hall, Virginia

Published by Betterway Publications, Inc.
White hall, VA 22987

Book design and cover by Julienne McNeer

Library of Congress Cataloging-in-Publication Data

Bodner, Richard A., 1942-
   Secrets of smart airline travelers

   Includes index.
   1. Air travel — United States — Handbooks, manuals, etc.
   2. Aeronautics, Commercial — United States — Passenger
traffic — Handbooks, manuals, etc.   I. Title.
HE9787.5.U5B63   1986   387.7'42'0973   86-18837
ISBN 0-932620-65-5 (pbk.)

Printed in the United States of America
0987654321

For my mother, Elaine, and late father, Charley H.

CONTENTS

CHAPTER 1

AIRLINE ALPHABET

How You Can Save On Almost Every Flight You Take... Without Restrictions!

The airlines use an alphabetical code on airline tickets to indicate how much you paid for your seat. By being aware of the codes, you can frequently save up to 60% and travel without restrictions.

The airlines love to advertise "No Lower Fares Anywhere," but when you walk up to the ticket counter or phone the airlines or your travel agent for reservations, you may not get the lowest fare. Example: We were recently in Portland, Oregon enroute to Seattle. I walked up to the Northwest Orient Airlines ticket counter and asked the price of a coach seat to Seattle on their next flight; answer $65! I then chose one particular letter of the alphabet — the letter "Q" — and asked if they had a "Q" fare available. Yes, they did! The same coach seat was now mine for only $45. Savings: 31 percent!! It pays to know your ABCs and your QMYDs when dealing with the airlines.

Let's get into the history of the matter a bit before I tell you exactly what to ask for to get the lowest price when you buy an airline ticket. Airlines are *very* competitive animals. Thht is why there are "Q" fares. They are also major purchasers of advertising, and subject to "truth in advertising" laws! In order to advertise: "No Lower Fare" or "Lowest Available Airfare" the airlines must prove to the government that they are telling the truth. Not necessarily every seat on each flight for which the fare is advertised need be priced at "The Lowest Available Airfare." Only a few at a low fare will satisfy government requirements. So basically what we've determined is:

➡ There are fares *lower* than coach
➡ These fares are on a limited seat basis
➡ The airlines will not necessarily offer you these fares — you've got to ask for them!
➡ These alphabet fares are frequently available with no advance purchase requirements

A rose by any other name — Q, M, OP, V, L, H, K — these are the letters of the alphabet that will save you money when you buy an airline ticket! What do they mean? If you ask one airline if they have a "Q" fare, they won't know what you're talking about. Ask them if they have an "M" fare and they will. Not all airlines use the same letter to indicate the same thing: they're allowed certain latitude in developing internal codes for their different fare structures.

Here are the fares you should request, and their decoded meaning:

H or **Q** or **M** :	Coach Economy Discounted
QN	: Night Coach Economy Discounted
L or **V**	: Thrift Discounted
K	: Thrift
KN	: Night Thrift Discounted
OFPK	: Off Peak

Remember, you should ask for these alphabet fares when you buy your tickets. You won't be laughed at by the airlines or your travel agent, in fact, they'll probably consider you a knowledge-able traveler and give you better service. Any time you can direct a ticket agent to exactly what you want, you are doing them and yourself a favor! In the San Francisco to New York market alone, there are over 32 different discount fares to choose from — all without advance reservation restrictions! It helps your travel agent or airline reservationist when you're specific!

There isn't one specific airline that always has the lowest fares between cities. For example, Continental is considered a low-cost leader between Denver and Los Angeles, but Continental,

Frontier, and United Airlines all have the lowest fare — if you know how to ask for it!

If you have access to an OAG (Official Airline Guide), you'll be able to determine the airlines that fly any particular route in the world. Another source for fare information is a relatively new publication called *Airfare Discount Bulletin* or ADB. This monthly compendium is available by subscription from ADB Publishing Company, P.O. Box 460, Riverside, CT 06878.

While we're discussing fares, there are some low-price options for international flights specifically for budget-minded vacationers. These are APEX and Standby. Standby means exactly what the word implies: you buy a ticket at a reduced price and get the "right" to standby for an available seat. Other than bargain charters, this usually is the least expensive way to travel. APEX is the other low-price option, but it has some restrictions. APEX means Advance Purchase Excursion fare. APEX tickets must be purchased from 14 to 30 days before traveling and usually require at least a seven-day stay at your destination. If you decide to change dates or flights there may be a surcharge.

A new addition to the "fare game" is Ultra Super Saver. This fare, introduced by American Airlines, and since copied by other airlines, can be as much as a 75 percent discount from the regular coach fare. But beware . . . your ticket may not be transferable to another airline, and if you cancel or miss your flight, you will be required to pay a stiff penalty: 25 percent to 50 percent of the ticket price.

With alphabet fares available at no penalty, one would be wise to consider using them instead of an Ultra Super Saver fare if there were any chance of a change in plans.

CHAPTER 2

CHARTER FLIGHTS

What You Need to Know!

C harter flights are the one area of air travel most subject to abuses. They are also one of your best air travel bargains. Charters can be a wise investment if you can be flexible and can accept the conditions that go with the purchase of a charter flight.

For years, unscrupulous tour operators have preyed on the public's desire for cheap flights. The ease of entering (and exiting) the charter business have made it a business ripe for abuse. It is not unusual to read about a planeload of passengers stranded in a European city during the busy summer season because the charter operator went broke. The only option left for the victims is to purchase a full-fare ticket back to the U.S. on a scheduled airline.

It is also *not* unusual for the Department of Transportation to receive complaints about charter flights that didn't operate after the unwitting victims had paid their money. There also are many complaints of cramped seating and long delays at some intermediate stop in Europe. The horror stories abound. But thankfully most charter operators do not share the reputation or tactics of the few bad apples who have besmirched the business. However, since it is possible for anyone with enough money to charter an airplane and offer package tours, it is advisable to take out insurance when you purchase charter tickets.

Tour operators charter both scheduled airlines and charter airlines. The main difference is seating comfort. Scheduled airlines' seating offers more legroom, an important consideration on long flights.

When purchasing a tour, whether operated on a scheduled

airline or one of the charter airlines there are some things you should definitely know:

➡ The tour operator or the airline may cancel any time up to 10 days prior to departure. The main reason tours get canceled is because they didn't sell enough seats to make a profit for the operator. This is a risk you take when purchasing a tour.

➡ Charter operators can change flight times and dates at any time prior to departure.

➡ Cancellation charges can be up to 100 per cent if you are unable to take the tour for any reason. The closer to departure time you cancel, the more money you'll pay in cancellation fees. Protect yourself by taking out an insurance policy.

➡ If the airline or tour operator cancels the flight, you may have to wait up to two months to get your refund.

➡ Tickets for tours are often not issued until the last minute — if then. Sometimes passengers are asked to pick up tickets or a boarding pass at the airport just before the flight departs.

➡ If your luggage gets lost, the tour operator may refuse to accept responsibility — another good reason to take out an insurance policy.

➡ Tour operators are allowed to increase the price of a charter tour up to 10 per cent at any time until ten days before departure. You either pay the increase or you don't get on the tour. Few tour operators offer any insurance to cover this contingency. It is advisable to set money aside to cover the possible price increase.

➡ If you have to take a scheduled airline to get to the tour's departure point and your scheduled flight is late or cancels, the charter flight won't wait. You could miss your flight *and* lose your money too. You would be prudent to have an alternate flight in mind that will get you to the tour's departure airport in case your scheduled flight is late or cancels.

Most travel agents can tailor a tour to individual clients and still offer greater savings and more flexibility. By booking two nights accommodations, transfers, or car rentals, you usually qualify for what is called an inclusive tour airfare, "IT" for short. The savings can be up to 40 per cent. If you don't find a tour package that appeals to you, ask your travel agent to check into an IT, then together you can create a tailor-made tour.

CHAPTER 3

COUPON BROKERS

What Are They and [When] Should You Use One?

A coupon broker is a person who makes a business of purchasing travel awards earned by frequent flyers. They resell these awards to the public and travel agents. Strictly speaking, coupon brokering is against airline policy — but not illegal.

Coupon Brokering is a relatively new business. Its shallow roots can be traced back to a promotion first used by United airlines in 1979. United wanted to rapidly regain market share after a costly strike by its mechanics. Those first few weeks after the strike they gave every passenger a coupon that could be exchanged for half price on any future United flight. This was a variation of the brand-loyalty strategy used successfully in the food product industry for everything from cereal to coffee. It made good sense: in those early days of deregulation most airlines only had a 50 percent load-factor. United was only giving away seats that [they thought] probably would have gone unfilled.

In the coming deregulated environment, airlines were infants in the world of marketing. Previously regulated by the CAB, routes and fares were usually determined by the government. If an airline wanted to raise prices they petitioned the CAB. Competition was also closely regulated by the CAB. After deregulation, airlines realized they had a lot of learning to do.

United thought coupons would create "brand loyalty" among their passengers. They also assumed that many of the coupons would never be redeemed; probably to rot in some desk drawer until forgotten. It must have come as a shock to airline executives working at Chicago's O'Hare airport that first day, greeted by this scene: entrepreneurs lining the concourse, hands full of $20 bills, imploring deplaning passengers to part with their coupons. Their cry, "Cash for your airline coupons," could be heard throughout the busy concourse.

They had just created a monster. Passengers were selling their coupons to the entrepreneurs, who later became known as "Coupon Brokers." Brand loyalty was not *the* compelling reason passengers had selected United airlines: Profit was! Thousands of coupons the airlines figured would rot in some desk or kitchen drawer were going to be used. And if they were all used the airline was going to lose revenue. Thanks to the coupon brokers, people who otherwise would have paid the airline full price for a seat were now going to pay half price. Airline revenue was being diverted right into the pockets of the budding brokers — a monster they had created.

Airlines seem to lack originality. If one decides to serve free champagne in coach, next week they'll all be serving free champagne. They don't even seem to be original with names; airlines used to be named "XYZ or ABC Airlines." New airlines have taken any reference to "air" completely out of their name; now they're not an airline, they're "Express": People Express, Midway Express, Florida Express. With such a penchant for imitation, is it any wonder then that, almost immediately, every airline in the United States had its own coupon offer? Competition among airlines is rough. If one airline comes up with a new marketing strategy, even if it proves unprofitable, the others feel they have to play the same game.

Other Airlines' executives only saw passengers being diverted to United airlines because of the coupon offer. They must have thought, "we can't allow them to give all those seats away, we've got to start giving our seats away too or we'll never make any money!" That, in a round-about way is just about how it all began. There have been refinements and perhaps the coupon offers are building brand-loyalty — for some airlines. One thing is certain, frequent flyers and coupon brokers are reaping the rewards.

It's been over six years since the first entrepeneur waved a fist full of $20 bills in the face of every deplaning passenger to start the Coupon Brokering industry. Airline frequent flyer programs and coupon brokering have matured. Coupons are no longer distributed in flight. Frequent flyer programs are now computerized by the airlines. To participate, one must enroll with each airline. Coupon Brokers no longer huddle in the concourses of major airports, they now operate from executive offices in major cities. The coupon broker ranks have thinned and marketing strategies have been developed. Coupon brokers now sell approximately 50 percent of their supply directly to travel agents.

SHOULD YOU USE A COUPON BROKER?

*T*here are definite advantages and disadvantages to using coupons purchased from a broker. If you fly first-class or business class, you can almost always save money by purchasing a coupon. For coach travel, your savings increase with the distance traveled. Generally, those traveling relatively short distances won't save anything using airline coupons. For flights less than 2,000 miles, airline promotional fares and low-cost airlines usually provide more savings.

COUPON ADVANTAGES:

➡ Savings of 25 percent to 50 percent off regular fares for First Class, depending on the length of your trip.

➡ Savings of 10 percent to 40 percent in coach on long flights.

➡ Free extras are sometimes included. Some coupons also entitle you to free hotel rooms and free rental cars.

➡ Occasionally a free stop-over in an additional city is included at no extra charge. For example: Some coupons would allow you to go from New York to Honolulu and stop-over in another city(s) on the return.

COUPON DISADVANTAGES:

➡ If you decide not to use your coupon you cannot get a cash refund (although some brokers will give your money back, they're not under any obligation to do so).

➡ Generally you must allow five to six weeks to receive the coupon in your name. If the airline delays the processing you may have to alter your plans.

➡ Tickets issued in exchange for coupons are only good on the issuing airline.

➡ Some coupons have holiday blackouts when they can't be used or other restrictions. Ask before you buy.

➡ Coupons generally have an expiration date, after which they cannot be used.

SOME BASIC RULES:

➡ Use coupons for First Class and Business Class Travel.

➡ Use coupons for coach travel on flights over 2000 miles.

➡ Never buy a coupon unless it is issued in your name (some airlines are starting to crack-down on unauthorized use of coupons).

➡ Ask if the coupon entitles you to free hotel rooms or free rental cars. This may make a coupon a better deal than a regular ticket at the same price.

➡ Ask if the coupon has any restrictions or blackouts.

➡ Make sure you know when the coupon expires.
NOTE: Coupon prices start falling the closer you get to the expiration date.

➡ If you have purchased a coupon from a broker or a friend, it is unwise to mention this fact to airline personnel, (most brokers will caution you accordingly).

NATIONALLY ADVERTISED COUPON BROKERS

The following coupon brokerage companies advertise regularly in the *Wall Street Journal, Frequent Flyer* magazine, and other publications read by business travelers. This list is strictly for the convenience of the reader and *not* intended as an endorsement.

The Coupon Bank	800-292-9250 USA
	800-331-1076 CA
The Horizon Group	800-892-2345 East Coast
	800-4-Flyers West Coast
American Coupon Exchange	714-644-4112
Travel Discounts Int'l	212-826-6644 New York
	312-922-3808 Chicago
Pricebusters	800-424-7849 USA
	619-275-6310 CA
Travel Mart	214-750-7600
Travel Enterprises, Inc.	212-691-6638 New York
AGCO	301-681-8200 East
	213-459-0404 West
The Flyer's Edge	312-256-8200
The Coupon Broker	303-759-1953

CHAPTER 4

BUCKET SHOPS

Outlets for Unrestricted Airfare Discounts

*I*f you want to tour Europe at the least expense, and if you can arrange your timetable with a certain degree of flexibility, here's what to do: buy a one-way (or roundtrip) ticket to London. When you arrive in London purchase onward tickets from a "bucket shop".

London is where you'll find the most bucket shops. The term "bucket shop" doesn't refer to the product they sell, rather to the fact that unsold tours and airline tickets are sold by this kind of business; sort of like putting the left-overs in a bucket so to speak.

Bucket shops are nothing new, in fact airline tickets and tours have been sold through this kind of outlet for years in London. Only since airline deregulation have bucket shops come into being in the United States. Typical U.S. "bucket shops" usually operate as "Discount Travel" clubs. Some require membership (and a yearly fee), others can be used at no cost.

Bucket shops all do basically the same thing: they market unsold tours and airline tickets to the public at a deep discount. About the most useless thing to a tour operator or airline is an unsold seat on a departing flight. Once the airplane takes off, the potential revenue for any empty seat is lost forever. The same with tours. Tour operators book and pay in advance for seats on charter or scheduled airlines. By booking a large block of space they are able to get a substantial discount from full price. In turn they "mark-up" their cost and sell the space to the tour purchaser.

Tour operators know that unsold space on a trip departing within a month or less is probably not going to be sold. The tour operator figures that it is better to get something for the unsold space so it is offered to a bucket shop. Often the purchase price paid by a bucket shop is less than 10 percent of the advertised full price of the flight or tour. The bucket shop negotiates such a deep discount that they can mark-up their price and still offer a discount to the public.

Several years ago some airlines started their own bucket shop sales. They introduced the "standby" fare. If seats were unsold at departure time, people who were standing-by at the airport could purchase them at a discount. Standby fares are typically offered on overseas flights.

In London, bucket shops keep their overhead low by operating from inexpensive walk-up locations. You'll find numerous bucket shop advertisements in the newspaper classified section (look for the Overseas Travel section). There are even a few with store front locations. But mainly you have to check the classified ads and phone a local telephone number. The best London newspapers to check for bucket shop ads are *The Guardian* and the *Evening Standard.*

A typical bucket shop ad might read like this:

> **Canary Islands — 1 wk incl. air** **£75.00**
> **Costa del Sol — 10-days 1st class hotel/air** **£65.00**
> **Depart Sept. 10, 17, & 30th.**
> **CALL US FOR LAST-MINUTE FLIGHTS TO CORFU, ATHENS, ZURICH, ROME AND AMSTERDAM. ALSO FLIGHTS TO THE U.S. FROM £99.00 ROUND-TRIP. PHONE 01-637-8485**

All you need to do is phone the number listed and inquire about the dates available for your destination. If you decide to purchase a flight, you go to their office and your tickets are written on the spot. Bring cash as most bucket shops do not accept payment by credit card.

Recently a delightful week on the island of Madeira including the round-trip flight, lodging at a first-class hotel and transfers sold through a London bucket shop for only £65.00. The full price if reserved in advance would have been at least £200.00 per person more.

Round-trip flights to Australia including free car rental were going for only £539.00. Flights to Spain were advertised as low as £49.00 and for another £30.00 you could purchase a week's accommodations. Daily flights to Frankfurt were selling for £66.

Bucket shops don't always purchase the land portion of a tour. You will find both flight-only as well as packages that include accommodations offered through bucket shops.

It is not unheard of to be able to buy a round-trip ticket to the U.S. for less than the one way U.S. price. If you plan to visit Europe more than once a year, you can pick up a cheap round-trip ticket from a bucket shop and use it for your return flight to the U.S. When you return to London you can again pick up another round-trip ticket to the U.S. Make sure that the ticket doesn't expire before you plan to return to Europe.

Bucket shops generally purchase the entire unsold inventory on a specific tour or flight. They count on their low prices to generate enough sales to guarantee a profit on their investment. Often bucket shops will put tours and flights that are just about to depart on sale. As the departure date gets closer, the bucket shop will lower their price for unsold merchandise. It is frequently possible to visit a London bucket shop in the morning and be on your way to some romantic European destination that same afternoon.

Since bucket shops deal in so-called distressed merchandise, not all destinations in Europe, the Middle East, Africa and the Orient are available at all times. Here's a list of the destinations most frequently available from London bucket shops:

Europe
Channel Islands
Lisbon
Maderia
Frankfurt
Rome
Milan
Venice
Zurich
Geneva

Costa del Sol
Majorca
Ibiza
Alicante
Malaga

Spain
Almeria
Madrid
Canary Islands

Greece
Athens
Crete
Mykonos

Far East
Tokyo
Singapore
Hong Kong Bangkok
Colombo
Jakarta
Peking
Seoul

Africa	USA & Canada
Tangiers	New York
Nairobi	Miami
Johannesburg	Boston
Cape Town	Chicago
Durban	Los Angeles
Madagascar	San Francisco
Mauritius	Vancouver
Seychelles	Montreal
Lagos	Toronto

As you can see from the above list, it's possible to see quite a bit of the world at cut-rate bucket shop airfares. Bucket shops operate openly in London, Brussels and Luxembourg. In the Far East the best deals are in Bangkok, Singapore and Hong Kong.

CHAPTER 5

OVERBOOKED FLIGHTS

Your Opportunity to Fly Free!

When you purchase any airline ticket (except a Standby ticket) the airline has an obligation to transport you to your destination on the flight you reserved. But the airlines have a serious problem with "No-shows": persons holding confirmed reservations who fail to use them and never notify the airline.

No-shows are an expense to the airline because they take a seat out of their reservations system which, theoretically, cannot be sold to someone else. When an airline flight takes off with empty seats they have lost the revenue that seat could produce. American Airlines calls it a "spoiled" seat.

Airlines now track historical data in their computers for each flight in their system. By studying this data they are able to determine the number of no-shows they can expect on each flight. They then use this data to make a calculated gamble on how many seats can be sold above the number of seats the airplane holds. Any seat sold after the reservations system indicates the airplane is full is called an oversold seat. Airline terminology: the flight is "oversold."

Occasionally everyone with a reserved seat shows up for a oversold flight and the airline loses the gamble. Then they're in trouble, and they will ask you for a favor! If you arrive at the departure gate with a reservation and there are no seats left on the airplane, you may have an opportunity to fly free!

How big a problem are "spoiled" seats to the airlines? American Airlines turned in the best overbooking performance in its history in 1984 yet they had 4,959,780 no-shows. The total number of no-shows boggles the mind when one remembers that there are at least two other airlines in the U.S. that carry more passengers annually than American — and American had the best performance according to figures compiled by the Department of Transportation.

Using computerized data, American was able to substantially reduce the impact of no-shows. American's planning paid off. They only experienced 198,991 "spoiled" seats (seats that departed empty on flights that had shown sold-out in the reservations computer). The value of those seats in lost revenue to American was $30,118,912.00.

When everyone with a reserved seat on an oversold flight turns up, the airlines ask for volunteers to give up their seats in return for transportation vouchers and seats on later flights. This is a standard practice among major airlines. If they don't get enough volunteers, things can get nasty for the hapless passenger agent. In 1984, American had 39,097 passengers volunteer to give up their seats. They also had 1,916 passengers classified as involuntarily oversold — these are the passengers that really cause trouble. Passenger agents fear for their lives when this situation arises.

I witnessed an involuntary oversold situation recently for a TWA flight from New York's Kennedy airport to London. As throngs of oversold passengers milled threateningly around the passenger agent, the offers to entice volunteers from the unruly crowd got better and better. Talk about good deals! On that flight the passenger agent raised the ante three times before he had enough "takers." The final offer: a free flight on TWA, positive space in first-class on the next London flight *and* $500.00 cash. Imagine yourself booked on that TWA flight. If you really didn't have to be in London at any particular time of the day you would have had the opportunity to fly free and put $500.00 cash in your pocket. How many persons volunteered to give up their seats when the passenger agent made his first offer? None! Perhaps they all thought that they absolutely had to be in London at the scheduled arrival time. The next TWA flight to London left a little over four hours later. In this instance *not* volunteering paid off —the ante was raised after each offer until the passenger agent had enought volunteers.

If you find yourself in this situation, "opportunity" has just knocked on your door. Don't answer right away if it looks like there are numerous oversold seats. Listen to the passenger agent's comments: phrases like, "way oversold," "I need another count," and asking other agents to "help with the processing" are dead giveaways that the flight is grossly oversold. If you notice this happening — don't take the first offer. If it appears that the flight is only oversold by a few seats and you can take the next flight without causing a disruption to your plans, then give serious consideration to the first offer. After all, others are reading this book too!

On flights in the continental U.S. the "offer" seldom gets to the point I witnessed on the TWA flight to London. It is most unusual for airlines not to get enough volunteers just by offering another free flight. United Airlines posts a sign at each check-in counter when there is a chance a flight might be oversold. The sign reads, "You may earn a free flight on United, just by taking another flight. Ask me for details." If you see this sign, there's a good chance the airline will ask you to fly free as a favor to them.

It is not too difficult to guess which flights have a chance of being oversold. The airlines aren't stupid. If their historical data indicates they can expect 50 no-shows on a particular flight, they will only oversell 50 seats. When you phone their reservations department they'll tell you, "sorry, that flight is fully booked." You then know the flight is probably oversold. Flights that are likely candidates for overbooking are Friday evening flights from major business centers and flights during busy holidays. If you want to play this game, reserve these flights whenever possible.

Here are the "rules" for playing the Fly Free game:

➡ Make reservations for flights that have a good chance of being oversold: any flight during Christmas or Thanksgiving holidays is a natural candidate unless you're going to East Podunk; flights on Friday evening from major business centers (best departure times are between 5:00 p.m. and 7:00 p.m.); flights to Europe (on a major airline) or Hawaii (on any airline) during February or the heavy summer tourist season, especially on weekends.

➡ Don't accept the passenger agent's first offer if it looks like he's ready to commit suicide.

➡ On flights within the continental U.S. be ready to volunteer for a later flight if you see certain signs on the check-in counter for your flight.

➡ Stay alert — ready to volunteer — and close to the passenger agent if it looks like only a marginal number of seats have been oversold on your flight. It's not considered "tacky" to volunteer to give up your seat before an announcement is made. Yours might be the only seat needed.

If you're one of the lucky ones to fly free, the airlines will love you. After all, you did them a favor!

If the situation arises where not enough passengers volunteer to give up their seats then the airline will have to "bump" passengers involuntarily.

Passengers who are involuntarily removed from a flight are frequently entitled to "denied boarding compensation." How much depends on the price paid for their ticket and how long they will be delayed in reaching their destination.

These are the rules established by the Department of Transportation to deal with involuntary removal (bumping) from a scheduled airline's flight:

➡ If the airline can arrange alternate transportation that is scheduled to get you to your destination within one hour of your original scheduled arrival time, you will not receive denied boarding compensation.

➡ If the airline arranges alternate transportation that will get you to your destination more than one hour but less than two hours* after your original arrival time, then the airline must pay you an amount equal to the one-way fare to your final destination — $200.00 maximum limit.

➡ For substitute transportation that will arrive at your destination over two hours* later than the originally scheduled arrival time (or if they fail to make any alternate arrangements) the denied boarding compensation is 200 percent of your ticket price or $400.00 maximum.

You always get to keep your original ticket and can have it refunded or use it on another flight at your discretion. Denied boarding compensation is payment for your inconvenience.

---

*The time limits are doubled for international flights.

There are a few exceptions and conditions:

➡ You must check-in at the gate before the airline's deadline. Deadlines vary from 10 to 90 minutes or longer as determined by the individual airlines (see Appendix G).

➡ You must have purchased your ticket before the airline's ticketing deadline; usually 30 minutes before departure.

➡ If the airline decides to use a smaller airplane than they originally planned for the flight, they're not required to pay denied boarding compensation to involuntarily bumped passengers.

➡ The charter airlines and charter flights operated by a scheduled airline are not included in the rules, nor are scheduled flights that are operated on airplanes that hold 60 or fewer passengers.

➡ International airlines inbound to the U.S. are also exempt from this Department of Transportation regulation.

CHAPTER 6

AIRLINE BANKRUPTCY INSURANCE

It's Probably Already In Your Wallet

If you had paid cash for a ticket on Continental, Air Florida, Braniff, Northeastern (or any other airline that went bankrupt), and hadn't used that ticket when the airline declared bankruptcy, then you probably were left holding the bag!

Bankruptcy insurance used to be offered free by some of the larger travel agencies to protect their clients in the event of airline bankruptcy. This kind of insurance is no longer available (at a reasonable cost) because insurance companies were getting hit hard with a number of claims from would-be passengers of bankrupt airlines. To add to the problem, airlines that were running short of cash would frequently advertise deeply cut bargain fares in an attempt to rectify severe cash shortages just before they declared bankruptcy. The bargain-hungry public would snap up these deeply discounted airline tickets and before they could use them, the airline declared bankruptcy and the hapless public was left with unusable tickets. Airline tickets on a bankrupt airline are usually worthless, unless one can find a collector crazy enough to want them.

There are three precautions to take — to avoid being taken:

➡ Don't pay cash for airline tickets.
➡ Don't buy airline tickets on an airline that hasn't started flying, no matter how good the "deal" may appear.
➡ If there are rumblings that an airline is in financial difficulty, don't buy a ticket on that airline unless you pay by credit card and have a back-up airline to take you to your destination.

The best bankruptcy insurance policy won't cost you a cent; it's your credit card. When you charge airline tickets to a credit card you can get your money back if the airline goes bankrupt before the tickets are used. Just contact the credit card company and follow their instructions to receive a refund or credit to your account.

Most airlines will accept payment by Visa, Mastercard, American Express or Diners Club. There is no extra charge for using your credit card. Visa and Mastercard will only charge interest if you fail to pay the charge within a certain time. American Express and Diners Club offer extended purchase plans for airline tickets to allow you to stretch out the cost. But if you pay your entire statement on time, there is no finance charge.

If you charged an airline ticket to your credit card and the airline went bankrupt before you used the ticket, Diners Club advises their cardholders to send them the unusable ticket via registered mail. Diners Club then contacts the airline and credits the amount of the ticket to the cardholder's account. American Express will also issue a credit to the cardholder's account.

As a general rule, if you notify the credit card company in writing within 60 days of the date that the unusable airline tickets appeared on your credit card statement, they should credit your account for the full amount paid.

Purchasing airline tickets by credit card has another advantage in the case of lost or stolen tickets. If the lost or stolen tickets are presented to the airlines for a refund, the airlines will not issue a cash refund. They are required instead to issue a credit to your account. In the case of a stolen ticket there is one exception to the above rule: airline tickets can be exchanged for another flight or a different itinerary and the value of the stolen ticket could be applied toward payment for the new ticket.

It is always wise to keep a record of the ticket number to make it easier for the airline to process your refund. When the airlines are supplied with the ticket number they may be able to issue an immediate replacement ticket. Without the ticket number, the airline may take up to six months to issue a refund, and if the ticket is used during that period the airline might refuse to issue a refund. Most will charge a handling fee for processing a refund.

The best self-insurance against airline bankruptcy, lost or stolen airline tickets is your credit card and your record of the ticket numbers charged to your card.

CHAPTER 7

BARGAIN AIRLINES

What To Expect!

Since airline deregulation in 1978, over 100 airlines have filed for bankruptcy or totally ceased operating. Although many of the airlines that failed were air taxi or feeder type operations, it is also interesting to note that sufficient numbers of jet low-cost airlines, charter airlines and two major airlines weren't able to survive. The two major airlines that declared bankruptcy came back to life as low-cost airlines, trying to fly their way out of Chapter 11 bankruptcy.

Deregulation created a new kind of airline known as a "low-cost" or so-called bargain airline. Bargain airlines typically start by flying leased airplanes in a small market segment. To gain media attention, cut-rate fares are offered —usually substantially less than those offered by carriers already flying the route.

Bargain airlines are able to keep their fares lower than major airlines because they usually don't have the high overhead — gates are rented from other airlines, maintenance is contracted out, and wages are lower because they aren't unionized. Over a period of time, their costs will climb and be reflected in higher ticket prices, but they can usually keep their fares below those of established airlines by offering less to the travelling public.

PeopleExpress airlines is a good example of a low-cost airline. They keep a tight rein on expenses, charging passengers to check baggage, and for onboard drinks and meals. From their headquarters in Newark, they have expanded their small original route system into a coast-to-coast operation, even flying to London from Newark. During their first few years in business, they didn't accept advance reservations; they couldn't afford the added expense of a computerized reservation system. People that showed up at the airplane first got on their flights. They built a reputation with, and developed a completely new segment of airline traveler — people who had never flown before now discovered they could afford air travel. The business traveler in general stayed away — they didn't like the uncertainty of the reservations system and being packed into seats jammed closely together to maximize the new airline's revenue.

Not all start-up bargain airlines have done as well as Peopl-Express. Some have gone bankrupt — leaving the public with worthless airline tickets. Others have taken advantage of the public's hunger for low fares and operated "scams" that have made the perpetrators rich while defrauding the public out of millions of dollars. One good example was an airline that never flew: Hawaiian Pacific. They ran advertisments in major newspapers offering flights to Hawaii at a future date for $99.00. The unwitting victim clipped a coupon from the newspaper and sent their check to Hawaiian Pacific. If they were fortunate even to receive a ticket, they weren't fortunate enough to get a flight to Hawaii in exchange.

Other abuses by airlines about to go out of business have taken the form of *extreme* bargain prices for purchase of tickets on future flights. This last-ditch attempt to raise money was used by Air Florida just before they declared bankruptcy. The same thing happened again with the "old" Continental airlines. When a low-cost airline goes bankrupt, chances are very good that no other airline will honor their tickets. In fact very few major airlines will honor tickets on bargain airlines — period. What this means is if you're holding a ticket on a bargain airline and the flight cancels, you will have to wait for another flight on the same airline, even if it doesn't depart for 24 hours. Even with all of their drawbacks, low-cost airlines have served the consumer well in today's deregulated environment. Major airlines have had to lower fares to compete — at least for the leisure market. And as the low-cost airlines come of age, they are offering more convenient schedules and more amenities to their passengers.

One should remember that the major airlines usually match the price of the low-cost airlines (on a limited seat basis). If you prefer to fly one of the major airlines, you can usually get the same fare offered by bargain airlines, but you will have to make reservations in advance to get the same low price.

LOW-COST AIRLINES

PeoplExpress	Braniff‡
Continental‡	Southwest‡
Transtar‡	America West‡
Midwest Express‡	Jet America‡
Presidential‡	Midway‡
Air Atlantia‡	IcelandAir†‡
Tower Air*	Mid Pacific Airlines‡
American Trans Air*	Sunworld
New York Air‡	PSA‡
Air Cal‡	Virgin Atlantic†‡
Transamerica*	Frontier
Florida Express‡	

OUT OF BUSINESS LOW-COST AIRLINES

Pride Air	Air Florida
Frontier Horizon	American International
Northeastern	Best Airlines
Air One	Hawaiian Express
Pacific East	Pacific Express
Arista	Galaxy
South Pacific Isl.	Global
Capitol*	Air Hawaii

*Indicates mostly charter flights
†Indicates international service
‡Indicates full-service

The greatest advantage to flying on a low-cost airline is price. While it's true that with a little advance planning the same low prices are usually available on major airlines (on competing routes), you can make last-minute reservations on the bargain airlines without paying a hefty premium.

The advantage to bargain airlines usually stops at price. Some (but not all) bargain airlines don't offer, or charge extra for the following services:

Meals
Coffee, juice or soft drinks in coach
Baggage check-in
Transfer of baggage between other airlines
Confirmed reservations

Bargain airlines usually reduce the pitch between seats. Pitch is the distance between rows of seats. The less the pitch, the more cramped the seating arrangements. This may be something you should consider when planning a long flight on a bargain or charter airline.

Overbooked or canceled flights occur on bargain airlines, too. When this happens on a major airline flight you will be put on the next available flight even if it is on a competing airline. This isn't usually the case on bargain airlines and it definitely isn't true on charter airlines.

The main service offered by any airline is transportation between two points. If price is your main consideration, you have two options: bargain airlines or advance purchase discounts on major airlines. The choice is yours.

CHAPTER 8

HOW TO HELP YOUR TRAVEL AGENT

Helping your travel agent is easy, and can be financially rewarding for you. The easier you make your travel agent's job, the greater your chances of getting exactly what you want at the lowest possible price.

A travel agent's job is not an easy one. Imagine that you're working on a giant jig-saw puzzle with literally thousands of pieces. There is no precise way to put the puzzle together; in fact, there are thousands of ways to complete the puzzle — all of them correct. Sometimes pieces of the puzzle are missing, other times if you put the pieces together as before, they won't fit. Does this sound like fun — insanity — work? Rewarding? You decide. Whatever you decide, the travel agent's job is all of these things. The thousands of pieces to the giant travel puzzle are located in two places: a document the size of the Yellow Pages for a large city, called the Official Airline Guide (OAG), and the Computer system on the agent's desk. These are the tools of the trade.

Travel options are so numerous today that many agencies hire several agents with special fields of expertise; vacations, overseas fares, tours and cruises. Some specialized agencies concentrate on only one aspect of travel or a particular clientele. For example, there are agencies that only accept corporate business and others that only sell cruises. The large full-service agency usually has personnel experienced in all aspects of travel.

In most cases the services of a travel agent are free. Airlines pay part of the ticket price as commission to the agency. Generally, domestic airlines pay 10 percent commission. International airlines usually pay 8 percent commission. If you reserve flights directly with the airlines, you pay the same price as you would at a travel agency but the commission that would have gone to the agency now goes directly to the airline. The consumer generally gains nothing and, in some cases, loses. Here's why: when you make reservations directly with an airline, the airline feels no obligation to tell you if another airline offers lower fares. A travel agent should have no such loyalty to any single airline and since he is working for his customer, most travel agents feel their obligation is to get their customer the best deal. To consider their commission ahead of their customer's budget would be false economy. It's a competitive business and travel agencies want repeat customers!

After covering operating expenses, a very well-run travel agency can expect to make no more than 2 percent to 3 percent profit on gross volume. Salaries are one of the major cost items in a travel agency. The amount of time a travel agent spends on each reservation can ultimately determine the profitability of the travel agency. If you can effectively communicate your *exact* travel needs to your agent, you'll get better service and better prices. Here's why: when you pinpoint exactly what you want, you are telling your travel agent where to concentrate his efforts. A narrower field of search means a more thorough search for everything available to fit your exact requirements.

Your travel agent doesn't expect you to know all of the available travel options, after all that's the reason he has a job. Remember though, only you know the things that can make your travel agent's job easier and you should share this information.

Communication is the key. If you're only looking for a second opinion, tell your agent — don't let him reserve your flight before you mention that you were just "window shopping." No one likes to go through a dress rehearsal then have the wedding cancelled!

If you ask your travel agent to check airfares, tours, or other travel services with the thought of getting ideas, let him know in advance. Your agent may be able to supply you with brochures and other helpful information to make planning more fun for you while giving you some money-saving options you didn't know were available. For instance, if your agent is aware that you plan a trip to Europe in a few months *and* you want the lowest airfare, he'll be able to look for inexpensive charter flights or advance purchase fares. If you let him think that you're interested in a flight in the very near future, he might not quote a discount fare with advance purchase restrictions.

Here is some of the information you should share with your travel agent to make your relationship profitable for both of you:

→ The exact dates you plan to travel.
   The further in advance you make reservations the more discount fare options are available.
→ The budget for your flight(s).
   If you want the least expensive airfare, say so in no uncertain terms. Believe it or not, this will help your travel agent.
→ The flexibility in your travel plans or dates.
   Flexible travel plans can help you save money. For example, a night flight is almost always less expensive than a daytime flight. If your travel agent is aware of your flexiblity, he can offer you this kind of money-saving option.
→ Your airline preference.
   If you are building frequent flyer credits on a particular airline, let your travel agent know. If you don't want to fly on a particular airline, let your agent know this, too.
→ If you're "window shopping" for ideas.
   Your travel agent may be able to tell you which airlines offer the lowest fare or direct you to tours, charter flights or offer free brochures to help you plan your trip.

Keep in mind that airline advertising usually emphasizes the lowest airfares. This can be extremely misleading. Frequently many qualifying restrictions are involved in getting the lowest fare. Also, the number of seats offered at the lowest fare are restricted. The earlier you book your flight, the better your chances of actually getting the advertised airfares. Even low-cost airlines have joined in the subterfuge by advertising their "off-peak" fares. If you ask your travel agent for the lowest fare and you don't get the price you have seen advertised, this doesn't mean that you've been cheated. More likely, it indicates that you weren't able to meet all of the qualifying restrictions or the limited number of seats at the advertised price had already been reserved.

When you find a good travel agent, stick with him. You'll find the relationship financially rewarding.

CHAPTER 9

MORE SECRETS

I n this chapter we let you in on some more time and money-saving tricks used by smart airline travelers. Things you can do to make life easier for yourself while you're at the mercy of the airlines.

No Smoking — Non-smokers now have more rights than ever before. In fact, until recently non-smokers had an airline that especially catered to them, Muse Air. While Muse Air (their name has been changed to TranStar Airlines) no longer has an *exclusive* no-smoking policy, airlines are required to give any passenger who requests it, a seat in the no-smoking section of the airplane. If more non-smokers show up for a flight than there are seats in the no-smoking section, the airline is required by law to designate additional rows of seats as no-smoking sections. This means the whole row, even if there is only one non-smoker seated in the row.

Curb-Side Baggage Check-In — At all of the major airports, porters for the airlines can check bags at curb-side. This saves you the effort of carrying your luggage to the check-in counter, and perhaps having to stand in long lines just to check your luggage. Tip the curb-side porters at least 50 cents per bag.

Airport Traffic Jams — When you're running late and you arrive at the airport only to find a traffic jam, some smart travelers will choose to get dropped off at the baggage pick-up (arrivals) area and walk up to the check-in (departures) area. This trick usually works unless you're traveling during a busy holiday such as Christmas when both arrival and departure areas of the airport will be jammed.

Boarding Passes — Your travel agent can issue boarding passes for most of the major airlines (and some of the regional carriers) when you purchase your airline tickets. Ask for the seat you want at the time you make your reservations. This saves you having to wait in line at the airport to check-in for seat selection.

Where* Not *To Buy Airline Tickets — Probably the worst possible place to purchase airline tickets is at the airport. There will be times when this is unavoidable (see chapter #1, Airlines Alphabet, to save money in this situation), but avoid this situation whenever possible. Travel agencies, and your own travel agent in particular, should be your first choice for purchasing airline tickets. These professionals know that if they don't get you the lowest fare, they won't get your repeat business. Ticket agents working at a busy airport counter are not inclined to find you the lowest fare. Their main goal (and many airlines monitor them for speed) is to sell the most tickets in the shortest amount of time.

Free Travelers Checks — Credit card companies want you to purchase their brand of travelers checks. The reason is simple; many people don't spend travelers checks immediately. This allows the credit card company to earn interest on your money. Diners Club cardholders who purchase Citicorp travelers checks can send the receipt for their purchase to Diners Club and have the 1 percent service charge credited to their account. Some travel agencies will also offer you free travelers checks to get your business. American Express travelers checks can be purchased without fee by members of AAA (American Automobile Assn).

Free Parking — At some major airports it may cost you more to ransom your car after a week's vacation than the cost of the airline ticket to go on vacation. In some major cities there are enterprising travel agencies located near the airport that will offer you free parking if you'll buy your airline tickets from them. Check your Yellow Pages and phone them before you buy from another agency. You'll find your tickets waiting for you when you arrive, a free parking place, and a free shuttle to and from the airport. Other large travel agencies will include one or two days of airport parking when you buy your tickets from them. It never hurts to ask: check the travel agency advertisements in the Yellow Pages. Check the local Yellow Pages advertisements for parking lots located close to the airport. These remote lots offer free shuttle service *and* lower prices.

Airline Clubs — If you travel frequently on business to and from major airports, then you'll probably benefit from joining an airline club. These clubs are open to anyone who pays the sponsoring airline an annual membership fee. Airline clubs are geared to the business traveler. Most clubs have a lounge area for relaxing, conference rooms (free of charge), telephones and an airline representative to help members with reservations and check-in. All offer free coffee and tea and bar service (some offer free cocktails too). Comfortable surroundings make clubs a pleasant place to wait for your next flight, while the airline representative will help with seat selection and other services. Selection should be made bearing in mind the airline having the most clubs in cities that you visit most often. It doesn't matter if you are flying on the airline club's airline. Once you belong to a club you can use it as frequently as you want. It's a good place to meet businessmen coming to your city for brief meetings. Clubs maintain a quiet atmosphere conducive to business. Listed on the next page are the airlines that have airport clubs, a price and service comparison is also listed along with the number of airports in which their clubs are located.

Lost Airline Tickets — Most airlines will refund your money if you lose your airline tickets, but the refund may take up to six months. If you've charged your tickets to a credit card, you'll have a record of the ticket numbers on your charge statement, making it easier for you to supply this information to the airline. If the lost tickets were purchased through a travel agent, the agent should complete a "LTA" (lost ticket application) form. When the form has been completed, you'll be asked to sign it and return it to the agent. If you purchased your ticket directly from an airline, you'll need to go to the airline to complete the LTA form. PeoplExpress, Southwest & Frontier airlines do *not* refund lost airline tickets.

SECRETS OF SMART AIRLINE TRAVELERS

Airline	Club	Fee/ Renewal	#Cities	Services
American Airlines	Admirals Club	$120/$70	21	B, S, T, MR, MS
United Airlines	Red Carpet Room	$125/$75	18	B, MR, S, *T C
Pan Am	Clipper Club	$120/$95	30	*B, C, S, T
Eastern	Ionosphere Club	$95/$70	28	B, MR, S, T
Delta	Crown Room Club	$85/$85	19	*B, S, T
Northwest Orient	Top Flight Club	$75/$50	17	*B, T, MR, S
TWA	Ambassador Club	$100/$100	26	MR, *B, T, S
Continental	Presidents Club	$105/$80	14	*B, MR, T, S
Piedmont	Presidential Suite	$75/$50	10	B, C, *T, S
Republic	Executive Suites	$50/$50	6	*B, MR, *T, S
U.S. Air	USAir Club	$65/$40	7	*T, MR, S, C
Western Airlines	Horizon	$105/$80	14	*B, *T, C, S

B = beverages served (* means free, including cocktails)

S = standard airline services; reservations, boarding passes, changing reservations, issuing tickets

MR = conference or meeting rooms usually available

T = telephone available (* means free local calls)

MS = message service

C = check cashing

Lost Or Damaged Luggage — If the airlines lose your luggage, they will make every effort to find it *and deliver it to you*. If you're away from home when they lose your luggage, some airlines offer a small cash advance to purchase immediate needs. If your luggage is never found, the cash advance will be deducted from the settlement offered by the airline. On domestic flights the airlines' maximum liability is $1,250.00. The airlines will negotiate to pay you any amount *up to* that limit. Don't expect to receive the maximum amount unless you declared a higher than normal valuation and paid the airline an additional charge when you checked your luggage. Airlines will almost always refuse to accept liability for cash, jewelry, and other negotiable items. Most travel agents sell an insurance policy to cover the loss or theft of your luggage. Airlines have been known to take up to three months before they give up trying to find lost luggage and offer a settlement.

If you discover that your luggage has been damaged by the airline, you should report it *before* leaving the airport. Insist on completing the airline's form before you leave the airport. Most airlines will repair or replace luggage that they damaged. The replacement settlement for luggage and contents is based on its depreciated value.

Airport Codes — The airlines have established three-letter codes for every airport in the world. When you check luggage, you should also check the three letter code on your luggage claim tag to make sure it matches your destination. Listed in the appendix are the three-letter codes for the major airports in the world. For example, if you're going to New York's Kennedy International airport, your claim check should have the three-letter code JFK. If it says LGA or EWR, your luggage is going to LaGuardia or Newark. Next time before you get on the airplane take a good look at the code on your luggage claim check. (See Appendix A for a list of three-letter identification codes).

Interline Baggage Tags — If you're going to change airlines, you'll get a different kind of luggage claim check. This rectangular claim check will list in reverse order, the airline, flight numbers, and destinations of your luggage, with the final destination and airline listed in the first position of the luggage claim check. They look like the example on page 46.

City Designator/Code

NOTICE

Exclusion From Liability. Liquids, fragile or perishable articles are transported at passenger's own risk.

TUL

TULSA OKLAHOMA

Printed in U.S.A. 10/84

Three-letter Destination

TUL

TULSA OKLAHOMA

Republic

Typical Baggage Tag for Non-Stop or Thru-Plane Service

Passenger Holds This Portion

This Portion Attached to Checked Baggage

Republic Airlines

BAGGAGE CLAIM CHECK

Baggage checked subject to tariff regulations and liability limits contained therein, unless excess value declared and applicable charges paid.

090-832

090-832

FLIGHT

TULSA OKLAHOMA

115

TUL

Republic

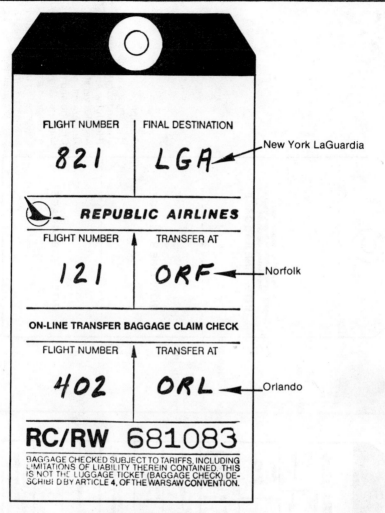

On-Line Baggage Tag

Example: Passenger boards Flt. # 402
in Miami for flt. to Orlando
then changes airplanes and
takes Flt. # 121 to Norfolk,
then changes airplanes to Flt.
821 to LaGuardia airport.

Note: On-line means that all
flights are on the
same airline; in this
example, Republic Airlines.

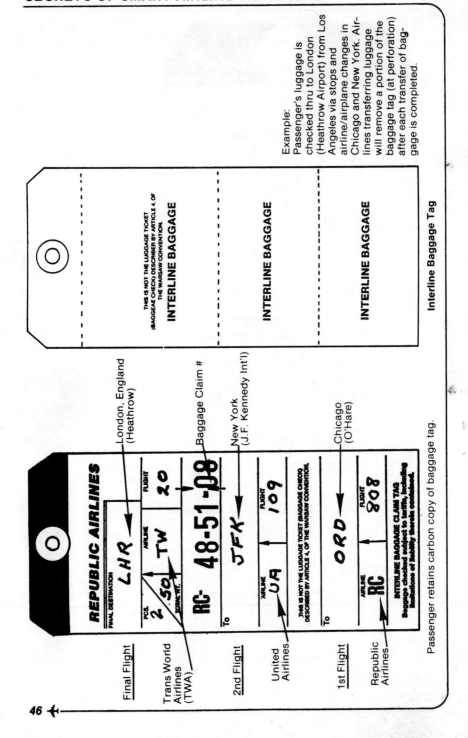

THIS IS NOT THE LUGGAGE TICKET (BAGGEAE CHECK) DESCRIBER BY ARTICLE 4 OF THE WARSAW CONVENTION.

INTERLINE BAGGAGE

INTERLINE BAGGAGE

INTERLINE BAGGAGE

Interline Baggage Tag

Example:
Passenger's luggage is checked thru to London (Heathrow Airport) from Los Angeles via stops and airline/airplane changes in Chicago and New York. Airlines transferring luggage will remove a portion of the baggage tag (at perforation) after each transfer of baggage is completed.

London, England (Heathrow)

Baggage Claim #

New York (J.F. Kennedy Int'l)

Chicago (O'Hare)

REPUBLIC AIRLINES

FINAL DESTINATION
LHR

AIRLINE   FLIGHT
TW   20

PCS.   TOTAL WT.
2.50

RC- 48-51-08

To
JFK

AIRLINE   FLIGHT
UA   109

To
ORD

AIRLINE   FLIGHT
RC   808

INTERLINE BAGGAGE CLAIM TAG
Baggage checked subject to tariffs, including limitations of liability therein contained.

THIS IS NOT THE LUGGAGE TICKET (BAGGAGE CHECK) DESCRIBED BY ARTICLE 4, OF THE WARSAW CONVENTION.

Final Flight

Trans World Airlines (TWA)

2nd Flight

United Airlines

1st Flight

Republic Airlines

Passenger retains carbon copy of baggage tag.

Throw-Aways — Sometimes the package price for a tour is lower than published airfares. Some smart travelers purchase a tour just to get the low-cost transportation. They don't use the accommodations included in the tour price. Enterprising individuals have been known to sell their "throw-away" hotel rooms (in Honolulu for example) upon arrival at their destination, effectively lowering the cost of their transportation even further. Your best source for low-cost tour information is the Sunday travel section of any major newspaper.

Senior Citizen Discounts — Several airlines have launched a concerted effort to gain business from senior citizens. Recent promotions include a $65.00 fare on one airline's flights for any senior citizens willing to travel on Tuesdays or Wednesdays. TWA and Eastern airlines have a yearly pass for senior citizens. Both programs have options to allow international travel. A companion pass is available for people under 65 traveling with the Senior Pass holder. The Eastern program also makes 50 percent discounts available at a number or large hotel chains. United Airlines' Silver Wings Travel Club offers passengers over 65 years of age a 10 percent discount on any airfare purchased on United. A companion pass with no age restrictions is also available.

Inter-Island Flights In Hawaii — Flights between islands in Hawaii can be relatively expensive; up to $42 each way. There are several ways to get a better price for inter-island flights. First, if you're bypassing Honolulu and plan to spend your entire vacation in either Maui, Kauai or the big island, Hawaii you can fly directly from the mainland, saving the added time and expense of inter-island fares. Second, there are usually empty seats on most inter-island flights to and from Honolulu and the inter-island airlines, Aloha, Hawaiian, & Mid-Pacific make these seats available at the last minute to standby passengers at greatly reduced prices. Third, Hawaiian Airlines now has flights to Honolulu from Los Angeles, San Francisco, and Seattle. Hawaiian's fare is no higher than any of the other major airlines, and if your onward destination is other than Honolulu, Hawaiian will throw in the inter-island flight for no additional charge. Fourth, the inter-island terminal is located quite a distance away from the international arrivals terminal. This can be inconvenient if you have carry-on luggage to transfer to another flight. Mid-Pacific airlines is the exception; they depart and arrive at the international arrivals terminal. Mid-Pacific's fares are usually the lowest of the three inter-island airlines.

Currency Exchange — Depending on the exchange rate trend for the U.S. Dollar, overseas purchases, including airline tickets give one the chance to make (or save) money by carefully examining available data about the exchange rate trend of the Dollar in relation to the currency of the destination country. Foreign denominated travelers checks can be purchased from major banks and from Deak-Perea Co. If the U.S. dollar appears likely to fall in value against the currency of the destination country, one would be wise to purchase travelers checks denominated in that country's currency. For example, if one is planning a visit to Britain and the trend of the Dollar against the Pound was down, then the Pound Travelers checks should be purchased to lock-in the prevailing exchange rate. On the other hand, if the Dollar is rising in value against a foreign currency, one should purchase travelers checks denominated in the U.S. Dollar and exchange them as needed while overseas. Better yet in this situation —charge purchases to a credit card. By the time the credit card company converts the foreign charge into U.S. Dollars, the dollar may have had a chance to rise even further, thus making one's purchases even less expensive than indicated at the time the sale was concluded.

Sold-Out Discount Seats — Capacity-controlled discount fares can frequently be purchased from large travel agencies, even when the airlines or smaller travel agencies show sold-out on their computer systems. Some large chains of travel agencies, such as Ask Mr. Foster and others, have unadvertised agreements with the major airline that supplies their computer system to make discounted fares available to their clients even if the normal allotment of capacity-controlled seats has already been sold. These discounted fares will only be available on the airline that supplies the computer system to the participating travel agency. For example, if a large travel agency chain uses the Apollo computer system supplied by United Airlines, then it may be possible to get a capacity-controlled seat on United through that agency, even though other agencies show only full-price coach seats remaining on the flight. This practice is not advertised to the public nor covered by written agreements; to do so would be to invite the wrath of other travel agencies who could not offer their clients the lower prices. Listed below are the airlines and the computer systems they supply to travel agencies. If you are planning to fly on one of the airlines below, it may be to your advantage to deal with a large travel agency that leases their computer system.

AIRLINE	*COMPUTER SYSTEM*
UNITED	APOLLO
DELTA	DATAS I & II
EASTERN	SODA
TWA	PARS
AMERICAN	SABRE

Selecting The Best Seats — Seating in the coach cabin of most airplanes is cramped at best. The airlines make more money by selling more seats on each flight, this is why you'll find seats on low-cost and charter airlines spaced even closer together. FAA safety regulations require all airlines to leave enough room for passenger emergency evacuation in the rows of seats located adjacent to an emergency exit. Most airplanes have at least two emergency window exits on each side over the wings. If you want more leg-room, request a seat in one of these rows. Seats in the rows just in front of the emergency exit row may not recline fully. The same is true for seats in the last row of the coach section. Ask for a bulkhead seat if you don't want to chance having a passenger in front of you reclining his seat into your lap. The only drawback to bulkhead seats is that there is no place in front of you for storing carry-on suitcases or briefcases.

Free Flight Insurance — Single-trip travel accident insurance usually costs $1.00 per $30,000 coverage when purchased at the airport. You can stop buying this kind of insurance if you charge your airline tickets to a major credit card. Here's why:

some credit card companies offer free flight and luggage insurance when you charge your airline tickets to their card. For example, if you charge airline tickets to your American Express card, you automatically get $100,000 in travel accident insurance and $1250.00 in baggage coverage; Carte Blanche gives you $150,000 coverage; Diners Club insures you for $650,000. Banks that offer the Gold Mastercard give you up to $500,000 free flight insurance plus $1250.00 insurance on your luggage when you charge tickets to their credit card. You may want to ask your sponsoring bank if their credit card offers you free flight and luggage insurance.

Freebies — More and more U.S. international airlines are offering free or reduced prices for accommodations and car rentals when you buy a ticket to Europe. Are they really a good deal when you compare the airfare on the major airlines to low-cost transatlantic airlines? Yes. Because of a complex system of international tariff regulations between countries, the freebies are a way of getting around the rules so the major airlines can compete. In late 1985 and 1986, Northwest Orient airlines offered free flights on their domestic route system for passengers flying Northwest to Europe during the off-season; TWA offered special tour packages, some including free car rentals, Pan Am offered free car rentals and there were other special deals by other airlines.

Even foreign airlines get involved in the battle for passengers, for instance, TAP Portugese airlines offered a week's free car rental anywhere in Portugal, ALIA Royal Jordanian airlines offered two-for-one fares during the low season.

To find out about these specials, look for advertisements in Sunday newspapers and in magazines or ask your travel agent. Although you may pay more for your ticket, the reduced prices and special "freebies" are a good deal for the consumer.

CHAPTER 10

SAVINGS ARE IN-SEASON

I f you're going to save money, knowing when to vacation goes hand-in-hand with knowing where to vacation. There are few vacation locations that don't have off-season prices. By avoiding high-season prices you can frequently cut the price of accommodations by up to 50 percent and take advantage of off-season airfares.

AIRLINE SALES

Since deregulation, airlines have had sales to boost cash flow during traditional slow travel periods. This practice is likely to intensify as airlines discover some of the marketing tactics retailers have used successfully for years. A good example of smart marketing are the bargain prices the airlines offer during the typically light load-factor days around Thanksgiving and Christmas holidays. For instance, airline statistical data shows that most seats are unfilled between December 24th and December 27th. If you'll start and finish your travel between these dates, the airlines will make it well worth waiting by offering discounts of up to 80 percent off the coach airfare.

FARE WARS

January through March are the slowest months for the airlines. With few exceptions, most airlines are unable to fill enough seats to show a profit in the first quarter. Therefore, they're all scrambling to get passengers during these three months. Fare wars are the result of their posturing to increase cash flow. Fare wars usually start after January 15th and extend well into March. Reductions can be quite dramatic! If you can plan to travel during this time period, you'll be able to get bargain prices on most domestic U.S. flights and flights to Europe. However, don't expect to get bargain prices to popular warm weather resort areas like Hawaii and the Caribbean. Fare wars to these areas usually start after September and run through the first week of December.

Fare wars can start any time a new airline or an existing airline starts flying or expands into new city pairs. New airlines generate free media publicity by offering ridiculously low fares. Existing airlines use the same ploy when opening up new markets. The airlines already flying the routes involved in the attack by new entrant airlines will usually match the promotional fares offered by the interlopers. Continental and PeoplExpress use promotional fares frequently, and the major airlines will usually match these fares for as long as they are offered by the new competition. The best source of advance information about the fare war's latest battleground is the newspaper. Watch for full page advertisements in the travel section of local newspapers or in the *Wall Street Journal*. Local and national news broadcasts on T.V. and radio are another good source of information about fare wars. In the winter of 1985-6 Continental was offering $99.00 one-way fares from Houston for the first 99 passengers on its new flights to London. This promotion lasted for two weeks.

Many people find that an off-season vacation offers more than just lower prices. Can you imagine, for instance, going to Florida or the Bahamas during high season and being faced with a cold-snap? Your vacation could easily be ruined by chilly weather you were trying to avoid. Postpone your vacation until later and you'll discover warmer weather and fewer crowds.

Vacationing during off-season makes sense in other ways, too. During the height of a resort area's season, rates are highest for rental cars, resort attractions — and you'll face crowds and rushed service at restaurants.

A frequent misconception about the Caribbean for example is that the island summers are unbearably hot. Not true. The difference in average temperatures in the Caribbean is only five degrees between winter and summer.

Winter in Europe can get very cold, but then you probably aren't going to Europe to sunbathe. Sightseeing during off-season; anytime from October 1 to June 1, makes sense. You'll see more, avoid the crowds, and pay less. If you want to vacation at some of the "hot-spots", wait until after the summer crowds of Europeans have gone back to work or head further south — Majorca, the Canary Islands or Malta.

Crowds at Colorado ski resorts disappear along with high prices right after Washington's birthday. This is when you'll find the warm spring skiing at its best.

Hawaii is a Caribbean parallel. The weather is rarely ever bad. Times to avoid in Hawaii are Christmas through January 2nd, the entire month of February, and when the kids are out of school for summer vacation (even though prices are generally lower during the summer months).

Vacationing during off-season makes sense in other ways, too. During the height of a resort area's season, rates are highest for rental cars, resort attractions — and you'll face crowds and rushed service at restaurants.

AREA	HIGH SEASON	LOW SEASON
Hawaii	Dec 15 - April 15	April 16 - Dec 14
Caribbean	Dec 15 - Apr 15	Apr 16 - Dec 14
Mexico	Dec 15 - Apr 15	Apr 16 - Dec 14
Florida	Dec 15 - Apr 15	Apr 16 - Dec 14
Europe	June - October	November - May
Ski Resorts	Dec 15 - Mar 31	Apr 1 - Dec 14
Palm Springs	Jan - April	May - Dec

Seasonal prices during Christmas are even higher in Mexico, Hawaii, and at ski resorts. After January 5, prices go down at most ski resorts until the 1st of February.

CHAPTER 11

SHOULD YOU ASK YOUR TRAVEL AGENT?

Ah, the glamorous life of a travel agent: free trips to exciting and romantic places, high pay, and inside information — right? Wrong! The life of a travel agent isn't a bed of roses, and as for the free flights to exciting romantic places, usually these are not really free. The average travel agent gets to go on vacation just about as often as the average blue collar worker. The myth that travel agents are highly paid is false. The average travel agent makes less money than a school teacher! So who benefits from all the "perks" the airlines bestow on travel agents? Usually it's the owner of the agency. This is a small reward for representing the airlines, to the detriment of the owner's pocket. The average travel agency shows less than a one percent profit! Most travel agency owners could do much better putting their money in a savings account rather than investing it in a travel agency, but the glamour of the travel industry is a magnet, and owners do reap many of the benefits, such as cruises at deeply discounted prices, free airline tickets, and familiarization trips at greatly reduced prices.

So when you ask your travel agent questions, try to remember that it just may be possible that you have more actual travel experience than your travel agent.

The list of questions asked of travel agents is as long (and sometimes ridiculous) as the list of airlines. Here are some questions *NOT* to ask a travel agent:

➤ Is the flight going to depart on time?

Travel agents don't have this information, it is available only from the airlines.

➤ What should I do if I miss my connection?

It's up to the airline and passenger to determine the answer to this problem!

➤ What kind of food is served on this flight?

Airlines don't furnish menus to travel agents. Don't ask anyway — you probably don't really want to know.

➤ Will my trip depart on schedule?

Only God and the airline know the answer to this one!

➤ Where is the nearest: bowling alley — hospital — drug store —souvenir store — hairdresser — etc.?

Chances are you'd have a better chance of getting an answer to these kind of questions from a New York taxi driver.

Travel agents are no more than representatives of the airlines, with extremely limited powers — the power to sell airline tickets. They can't change the scheduled departure times of flights, they can't reinstate cancelled flights, they can't find lost luggage, they can't guarantee smooth weather, and they can't do anything for you if your flight cancels.

Your travel agent should be able to give you advice about places they've personally visited. Ask specific questions, and ask the travel agent if he has personally visited the areas or taken the trip you've planned, before you take his advice. Many travel agents get their information from the same brochures that are available to the public. Here are some questions your travel agent should be able to answer:

➤ What kind of airplane will I be traveling on?

Travel agents have this information readily available in their computer system.

➤ Is there any penalty if I change or cancel my reservations?

A travel agent should inform you, or place a notice with your ticket if the fare has a penalty for cancellation or changes.

➡ What is the airline's policy in case I lose my tickets?

Although most airlines will refund lost tickets, some of the low-cost airlines won't. Your travel agent knows which ones.

➡ How far in advance do I have to check-in for my flight?

Your travel agent should be able to tell you the airline's specific check-in requirements.

➡ How far in advance do I have to purchase my ticket?

Some fares require advance purchase of anywhere from seven days to three months. Make sure you know how far in advance purchase is required. If you miss the deadline, you may be forced to pay a substantially higher fare.

➡ Can you issue my boarding pass with my tickets?

Some automated agencies can issue boarding passes and save you a long wait at the airport seat selection counter.

➡ If the fare increases before I leave, will I have to pay more for my flight?

Most airlines will not pass a fare increase on to passengers who have already been ticketed. Your travel agent can advise you of the airline's policy.

➡ If the fare goes down before I travel what should I do?

Your travel agent can tell you how to get your tickets rewritten for the lower fare. You might want to ask your travel agent if they automatically advise their clients in this case.

Some people take revenge on their travel agent if an airline mistreats them in any way. Try to remember that once you've purchased your airline ticket, you're at the mercy of the airlines and all your travel agent can do if things don't go right is offer you a shoulder to cry on . . . if he has time.

CHAPTER 12

ROUND-THE-WORLD FARES

Buy a ticket around the world! "Do you think I'm made of money?", might be your response to your travel agent's suggestion. But independent travelers have discovered that a "round-the-world" fare can be less expensive than an APEX fare - depending on the distance you travel, and the number of cities you plan to visit.

A substantial number of international airlines offer round-the-world fares but that doesn't mean that you're limited to just one airline for all flight segments. Some airlines operate an "interchange" so that you're able to use a combination of airlines to get where you want to go.

Round-the-world airfares can cost much less than individually priced APEX tickets *if* you're planning to stop at a number of cities, for instance a trip from San Francisco to Cairo with stopovers in London, Geneva, and Athens. Or a flight from New York to Hong Kong with stopovers in Los Angeles, Honolulu, Fiji and Tokyo. The reason round-the-world fares are less expensive in this case is because most APEX or Super APEX fares don't allow stopovers. With an APEX priced ticket, even though you may have to stop in a city to change airplanes, you're not allowed to spend time visiting the stopover city before continuing your trip.

In our first example, San Francisco to Cairo with intermediate stops, once you reach Cairo you would have to continue your journey in an eastbound direction. In other words, backtracking is not allowed with round-the-world fares. Once you start your trip you must continue to travel in the same general direction until the trip is completed.

Unlike many APEX and economy fares, round-the-world fares usually have a much longer time limit: tickets are valid for six months on most airlines, and a few airline combinations allow a full year to complete the trip. There are some other advantages too: the first leg of your trip is the only flight that needs to be confirmed in advance. Once you've made reservations for the first flight of your journey you can leave the rest of the legs of the trip "open" and make reservations as you choose.

Before you rush out and purchase a round-the-world airline ticket there are several things to remember — about the rest of the world's level of airline service. Most Americans & Europeans are used to having frequent service between popular vacation and business destinations. The level of service is most often dictated by the number of airlines providing flights in a certain market. If only a few airlines provide service on a route, say Karachi, Pakistan to Singapore for example, you can expect the number of flights between the two cities to be much more limited than flights between New York and London where the competition is fierce. In parts of the world, Africa in particular, it is not unusual to have only one flight per week between certain countries. The reason is because a lack of passenger traffic between some less popular destinations would make more frequent service unprofitable.

A round-the-world flight takes both planning and time. To allow anything less than three weeks to complete the trip is considered foolish by most seasoned world travelers. Selecting the airline(s) is probably the most important (and possibly difficult) part of the planning process. You'll need the help of a good travel agent when you're ready to decide which combination of airlines to use for your planned itinerary.

Round-the-world airline tickets can be purchased for as little as $1990 for coach economy seats; $2899 for business class; and $3799 for first class. In order to make a price comparison between a round-the-world fare and a series of economy fare tickets your first decision has to be which cities you want to visit. Once you have made this decision it will be easy for your travel agent to help you select the airlines you'll have to use to make the trip. It's more than likely the cities you plan to visit will determine which airline combination will make it possible to complete your planned itinerary on a round-the-world ticket. For example, if you wanted to depart from Los Angeles and stop in New York, London, Frankfurt, Athens, Singapore and Hong Kong you could choose a combination of United Airlines/British Airways or TWA/Singapore Airlines. The same trip would not be possible on a Northwest Orient/Air France combination because stops in Frankfurt, Athens, and Singapore are not eligible destinations on their round-the-world airfare.

Round-the-world travelers are restricted by the airline combination they choose. Once tickets are purchased on a particular airline combination, flights can only be on the airlines in that combination. This is why airline selection is so important when choosing a combination for your round-the-world journey. If your trip will involve stops in cities the airline in your combination doesn't serve on a daily basis, you may find yourself stranded between flights unless you're willing to pay extra to take the next flight on another airline. Once you've made your selection of airline combinations for your round-the-world trip, it's a good idea to get the complete flight schedule for the airlines you'll be using. Flight schedules are usually available at the airline's airport or city ticket offices. If that isn't convenient, you might want to phone the airline's nearest office and request they mail a current schedule to you.

Depending on the exchange rate for the U.S. dollar, you may be able to save even more money by purchasing your round-the-world tickets for flights originating in a foreign country. While tickets purchased for departures from the U.S. must be priced in dollars, if you were to start your round-the-world flight from England, the Netherlands or Belgium, your travel agent or the airlines can sell you tickets based on the foreign currency exchange rate prevailing on the day you purchase your ticket. If you decided, for example, to purchase a round-the-world ticket from London, and took a low-cost airline from Newark to London, you would be able to cut the cost dramatically. If the Dollar-Pound exchange rate is $1.50 to 1 Pound and the round-the-world economy fare from London is 1050.00 Pounds, your round-the-world ticket that would cost $1990.00 in the U.S. would cost $1575.00 in London. Adding the $189.00 one-way fare from Newark to London on PeoplExpress or Virgin Atlantic airlines brings your cost to $1794.00, a savings of $196.00. When you complete your round-the-world trip in the U.S., you would still have a ticket to London that could be used any time before its expiration date. If you don't like the idea of flying round-the-world in a coach seat, consider purchasing a business class seat; in London or the Netherlands the cost would be slightly more than an economy class seat purchased for departure from the U.S.

Round-the-world flights require a great deal of work on the part of your travel agent. According to *Consumer Reports Travel Letter*, there are more than 33 different combinations of airlines that could provide round-the-world flights for departures from U.S. cities. There isn't any convenient reference material a travel agent can consult to give you an immediate answer to your question about the best airline combination to use for your round-the-world itinerary. Different airline combinations and whether you choose a westbound or eastbound itinerary, determine both the price and the airlines available to fit your planned itinerary. The best help you can give your travel agent is to make certain you have identified all the cities you plan to visit before you call to ask for a price quote. If you decide to change your itinerary after your travel agent has located an airline combination that flies to all the cities you want to visit, your travel agent may have to start the search all over again.

Consumer Reports Travel Letter did comparison shopping for round-the-world fares in its January 1986 issue. Their study covered South Pacific westbound routings and North Atlantic eastbound routings. The article has a useful table of major U.S. and foreign cities and the airline combinations that serve them. If you're planning a round-the-world trip you can purchase this issue by writing to : Circulation Director, *Consumer Reports Travel Letter*, 256 Washington St., Mount Vernon, NY 10053. The cost is $5.

As a general rule, if you've planned a long international trip with stops in more than two or three foreign countries, you should compare the price of a round-the-world ticket to the cost quoted for your roundtrip flight.

CHAPTER 13

WHEN YOU GET THERE

Accommodations — You Can Get A Discount Almost Everywhere!

Travel clubs, corporate rates, senior citizen discounts, bucket shops, American Automobile Association, even travel agents offer discounts on accommodations in the U.S., Orient, and Europe — other destinations, too. Take a package tour or combine your airline ticket purchase with the purchase of a hotel room and you'll end up getting a discount on the whole package. In short, very few people ever have to pay "rack rates." There are even some good ways to find luxurious accommodations; villas, condos, private homes at a discount.

Some hotel deals even work in reverse: a consortium of luxury hotels was offering a free round-trip ticket to Europe for spending any eight nights during the year in any of their hotels: the catch was that you had to pay full rack rates, but this still works out to a hefty discount when you deduct the price of a round-trip ticket to Europe! Or take advantage of some of the off-season specials offered by airlines on European routes and get everything from hotels to rental cars at a deep discount.

Let's cover the various ways to get discounts on accommodations:

MAJOR TRAVEL CLUBS

➡ AARP (American Association of Retired Persons) offers discounts of 10 percent to 50 percent at the major hotel/motel chains.

➡ AMOCO's International Travel Card and ENCORE offer a second-night-free program at approximately 1500 hotels/

motels. Few of their offerings are in Europe or popular resort areas, and some of the discounts are limited to weekends or off-season.

➡ AMERICAN AUTOMOBILE ASSOCIATION offers discounts of 10 percent or more at hundreds of hotels/motels.

➡ CLUB COSTA offers discounts of 10 percent to 50 percent at hundreds of [mainly luxurious] resort properties; these tend to be in condos or private rental villas and cottages and seem suited more to families. They also offer corporate rates at Westin, Stouffers, and Howard Johnson's hotels/resorts. In Europe they have an associated agency that discounts hotels to 40 percent in the major European cities.

➡ INTERNATIONAL AIRLINE PASSENGERS ASSOCIATION offers up to 50 percent off at higher-priced hotels worldwide. The discount is year-round and not limited to off-season.

TRAVEL AGENCIES

Many travel agencies belong to consortiums that offer corporate rate hotel discounts to the agency's customers. There are more than five major consortiums that make this kind of discount available. Check with your travel agency to see if they belong to a consortium.

SENIOR CITIZEN DISCOUNTS

There are several national hotel/motel chains that offer senior citizens at least a 10 percent discount: Travelodge, Rodeway Inns, and Ramada Inns and other chains offer senior citizen discounts.

BUCKET SHOPS

There are discount travel agencies and hotel bucket shops in Europe and the Orient that offer up to 50 percent discount at hotels. The catch here, at least in London, is that the discounts can only be offered to foreigners — just perfect for American tourists! Some of the better-known hotel bucket shops in London are: *Room Centre* - ph. 01-328-1790 — (8 percent - 20 percent off) at thousands of hotels in Europe; *Value-Travel* - 01-404-4883 –- (up to 50 percent off) at hotels in the U.K. and Europe, although not quite as large a selection; *Superbreak* - 01-278-

9646 — good prices for accommodations (usually include breakfast and dinner) in older hotels in the U.K. located outside London. In Bangkok try *Chawla Travel & Trading Co. Ltd.* - Ph. 233-4328 — for discounts of 35 percent to 50 percent off regular prices. Visitors to other countries in the Orient report being able to get a discount just by asking at check-in.

CORPORATE RATES

Almost every hotel/motel chain offers a corporate rate program. Sometimes the corporate discount is substantial, other times it's just a "token" amount. Any company can apply directly to the headquarters of the hotel/motel chain for a corporate rate card or to be entered into the chain's computer system of companies eligible for corporate rates. Some people have written directly to hotel corporate offices on stationery they've purposely created to use in obtaining corporate rate discounts. Others have been known to mention that they are with a nationally recognized company when they check-in and have been offered corporate rates without any form of personal identification proving their employment claim.

ON YOUR OWN

Newspapers, magazines, private newsletters, even company bulletin boards can be a good source for locating discounted accommodations. Private owners of resort properties frequently decide to rent their accommodations by themselves when they're not using them. Management companies in the top resort areas frequently charge up to 50 percent commission for providing rental service. By avoiding this kind of management fee, private owners can afford to rent their accommodations directly to the public at a discount. Check the classified section (Resort/Vacation Accommodations) in the following newspapers for direct-from-owner discounts: USA Today, New York Times, Chicago Tribune, Los Angeles Times, Boston Globe, Miami Herald (and just about any leading newspaper in a major city). Private newsletters such as *International Living, Island Properties Report, AOPA Pilot, Airline Pilot Magazine, Trade-a-Plane*, and others always carry advertisements for rental properties. Magazines to check: *Texas Monthly, San Diego, Los Angeles, Travel/Holiday, Aloha, Private Pilot, Flying, Sunset.*

CHAMBER OF COMMERCE

The chamber of commerce in most resort cities maintains a list of accommodations available to visitors, some at substantial discounts. Just address your request to the chamber in the city(s) you plan to visit.

RACK RATES

Rack rates are the rates hotels, motels, and resorts will quote if you phone directly or arrive without a reservation. All discounts are from rack rates. If you find yourself in a situation where all you can get are rack rates, you may be offered a choice between three or more categories; standard, deluxe, or superior. With few exceptions, the main difference between rooms in each category is nothing more than its location. In high-rise hotels the standard category rooms are located on the lower floors, superior rooms on higher floors or with better views. Usually the rooms are the same size. If you're just interested in a place to sleep, you'll save money by taking a standard category.

With a minimum of advance planning, you can avoid paying full rack rates for accommodations, even in season.

CHAPTER 14

CHEAP FARES RESTRICTIONS

Read the "Fine Print" First!

Airlines have many different names for promotional fares: Super Saver, Easy Saver, Super Apex, Standby, Ultra Super Saver and more. These are the fares you'll see advertised in newspapers, but note the small print, "some restrictions apply" or the word "from" immediately in front of the price.

Many travel agents wish the words "from" or the phrase, "as low as" could be banned from airline advertising. Consumers tend to miss these "catch" words and phrases when they browse through the Sunday travel section of major newspapers and discover that it's possible to go to Hawaii or the Caribbean for "as low as" $99. By the same token, it's frequently frustrating or outright disappointing to find that the restrictions placed on these bargain fares are almost as long as the Congressional Record, and to get the advertised fares you need to make your reservations as much as a month ahead of time. Guess who gets the blame when the consumer is told that the bargain fare he read about in the paper doesn't apply to him? Right, — the poor travel agent!

The lowest advertised fares are what is commonly referred to by the airlines as "promotional" fares. They are aimed at the vacation travel market. Restrictions are placed on these fares to make them unavailable to business travelers who frequently travel without the opportunity to plan trips in advance. Until recently, full-fare business travelers made up the majority of the airlines' business: their bread and butter customers. Vacation travelers, filling otherwise empty seats, became the cake and ice cream! Promotional fares benefit the airlines three ways: additional cash flow, advance bookings and higher load factors (the percentage of seats occupied). The proliferation of low-cost airlines has benefited the consumer by creating competitive pressure on the major airlines' promotional fares. Many of the restrictions on promotional fares have been reduced, or in isolated instances such as fare wars, removed. Major airlines are now finding that passengers traveling on some type of promotional fare account for the majority of their business.

Large corporations' travel departments have learned how to use the system to their advantage, too. By studying the travel patterns of their employees who regularly travel on business, they're able to book some promotional fares far enough in advance to realize substantial discounts from the full-fare prices. The average consumer isn't fortunate enough to have a corporate travel department looking after his interests, so he must rely on his travel agent to explain the promotional fare restrictions or read the "fine print" in the airline advertisements.

Individual airlines don't always use the same exact name for identical promotional fares offered by other airlines, even though they may have the same restrictions. For example, Ultra Supersaver and Ultimate Supersaver usually have the same restrictions and cancellation penalties when they are offered by different major airlines. To help you get through the maze of restrictions and penalties, some of the most commonly used terms to describe the different promotional fares are listed below.

Ultra Super Saver and **Ultimate Super Saver:** Must be ticketed at least 30 days prior to departure but not later than two weeks after making reservations. Minimum stay over the first Sunday and maximum stay of 21 days. 25 percent cancellation penalty.

Budget Fares and **Discount Coach Fares Q, Q9, B9, M, K, OFPK:** No specific rules or cancellation penalties. The number of seats available is capacity-controlled by the individual airlines.

APEX and **Super APEX:** These fares have a 20 to 30 day advance purchase requirement. Minimum stay can be from 4 to 14 days and maximum stay can be up to 6 months (depending on the country visited). They may have varying cancellation charges.

Easy Saver: 7-day advance purchase required. This fare is better than full-fare coach but definitely not one of the best promotional fares.

Late Saver: Almost the same as a Standby fare, but some airlines will sell this fare up to 3 days before departure.

Check the advertisements carefully for the "fine print" before you phone your travel agent. If you want to take advantage of the savings promotional fares offer, you must meet the restrictions and be willing to accept any cancellation penalties that go along with the fares. Airlines offer the best discount promotional fares on Tuesday, Wednesday, Thursday, and Saturday to get you to fill empty seats on days when business travel is lightest.

CHAPTER 15

SHOULD YOU JOIN A TRAVEL CLUB?

T here are many reasons why you should join a travel club, and some good reasons why maybe you shouldn't. The main reason anyone should join a travel club is to save money. The reason you wouldn't want to join a travel club would be if you couldn't find one that fit your travel patterns, or you don't travel enough to make the membership fee worthwhile.

Most travel clubs offer a money-back guarantee. This gives you the opportunity to try them without risk. If you're not satisfied during the trial period, you can get your money back. The benefits of the established travel clubs are summarized at the end of this chapter.

If you don't travel frequently enough to make use of the benefits of a travel club, then you would do better to save your money. There are travel clubs that publish good travel magazines filled with interesting articles and travel tips that are worth joining just for the entertainment and educational value. One should weigh the advantages and discounts each club offers before making a decision. Some clubs appear to offer a multitude of services and benefits, but it is wise to read the "fine print" in their literature before you make your decision to join. Often the words "up to" are used before the exaggerated discount claims. When you see these words used, beware, frequently the majority of the discounts offered are less than the percentage that follows the words "up to."

If you usually travel on business, then you'll want to choose a travel club that offers discounts on accommodations, airfares, and car rentals in the cities you usually visit on business trips. If you travel mainly on short notice, then the exaggerated claims of significant savings on airfare can be misleading. No matter what a travel club claims in their brochures, it is the airlines that set prices for airline tickets. Most discount airfares involve some kind of advance purchase requirements specifically geared to the vacation traveler who can make plans to travel during off-peak times or in the middle of the week. Other discount airfares involve the use of charter flights that usually don't operate frequently enough to be used for business purposes. Almost anyone can get a discount from the full coach fare by using the information covered in this book in the Airline Alphabet chapter. It's not necessary to join a travel club to get these fares.

There are a number of travel clubs that offer "last minute" discounts. The savings offered by these clubs are substantial, but while their advertisements have great appeal, one must analyze the value in this kind of travel club. These clubs act as a clearing house for tour operators. They sell the remaining unsold space on charter flights and tours when it appears that the tour operator will not be able to sell the space at the full price. Club members can save up to 60 percent off the full price and the travel club and tour operator make money on the deal, too. If you have a spirit of adventure and time to wait for exactly what you want, these clubs can offer significant savings. But if you're limited to when you can vacation, or on a specific budget, or have specific ideas about where you want to vacation, then these clubs may be of limited value. Most tours depart from three major East Coast cities: New York, Philadelphia, and Boston. If you don't live near these cities, you'll face the added expense of transportation to and from the departure city, often without enough time to take advantage of the airlines' advance purchase discounts. Conceivably, you could wind up spending the money you saved on your charter flight in higher full-fare airline tickets. Ideally, the last-minute clubs should appeal to retired people living near the major departure points mentioned above. If you have specific tastes in the selection of accommodations, this kind of club could be a disappointment. Frequently, tours use less expensive rooms in hotels — the ones with the worst views — or budget accommodations that you might find unsuitable. Ask questions before you commit money to this kind of club.

Another benefit of joining travel clubs is a discount on car rentals. While this can save a business traveler a substantial amount of money, the vacation traveler can usually do just as well by booking in advance with the major rental companies or using some of the smaller budget rental car concerns located in most major resort destinations. Even with a discount from the major car rental companies, Hertz, Avis, or National, you'll still be able to beat their discounted price by renting from the smaller rental companies such as Thrifty, American International, Snappy, and Payless/Holiday.

Some travel clubs function as consumer rights organizations and outlets for low-cost flight and travel insurance and little more. You can frequently spot this kind of travel club by their advertisements with no specific benefits mentioned except the insurance they offer as a part of membership. Flight insurance is considered by many to be the worst kind of insurance purchase. The odds of being killed on a scheduled airline are so low as to make a roulette bet in Las Vegas look like a sure thing.

At least one other travel club offers an impressive number of motels and hotels in a discount program with the second night free. It is possible to realize 50 percent savings on accommodations through this club if you stay in a hotel for two nights, then move to another for two nights, etc. While many of the hotels/motels in their program have no restrictions, some of the properties in resort areas limit their participation to off season and weekends only.

If a travel club advertisement offers you *up to* 70 percent off on airfares, be a little dubious. What they may be offering is nothing more than the usual advance purchase airfares available on almost every airline. Contrary to popular belief, it is the airlines that set airfares, not travel agents or travel clubs. If a travel club promises to give you over a 10 percent discount on airfares, they are usually basing their claim on advance purchase or excursion fares. The standard commission paid to travel agents is 10 percent for domestic flights and 8 percent for international flights. Some tour operators and wholesalers are able to purchase blocks of space from the airlines and get a lower price, but it would be financially impossible for them to purchase blocks of seats on flights to every destination. Again, if they offer what you want *when* you want it, then you're in luck and your travel club membership will pay off. But, for example, if you want to vacation in Hawaii during Christmas or the month of February, and your travel club hasn't managed to secure blocks of space, then you're not going to get that discount you imagined after you read their brochure. It's as simple as that.

Another recent development since deregulation is the travel club that shares their commission on airline tickets and tours. Usually these clubs don't advertise the spectacular savings offered by the last-minute clubs, but if you travel frequently or like to plan your trips in advance these clubs offer significant savings. Beware though of the clubs that offer a credit toward a future trip. If you only take a few trips a year, you may never be able to cash in your credits. Travel clubs that rebate a portion of their commission may advertise, up to 50 percent commission returned to you. What this means is that you'll get up to 5 percent of the price of your airline ticket back — usually in a check. There is one travel club, ADCI/Club Costa that doesn't play games with their advertising. They flatly state that they guarantee at least 5 percent cash back when you buy your airline tickets from them. Although their claim doesn't sound as impressive as the clubs that advertise *up to* 70 percent off on airfares, ADCI/Club Costa can discount any fare available on scheduled airlines — even the advance purchase fares that are already 70 percent off the regular full-price fares.

Some of the major travel clubs and their membership fees are:

FEE	CLUB NAME
$45.00	STANDBYS — (313) 352-4876
$40.00	DISCOUNT TRAVEL INTERNATIONAL — (215) 878-8282
$25.00	AIRHITCH/WORLDWIDE DESTINATIONS UNLIMITED — (212) 864-2000
$20.00	ACCESS* — (212) 333-7280
$30.00	LAST MINUTE TRAVEL CLUB — (617) 254-5200
$35.00	MOMENTS NOTICE — (212) 486-0503
$45.00	WORLDWIDE DISCOUNT TRAVEL CLUB — (305) 534-2082
$49.00	ADCI/CLUB COSTA — (800) 225-0381

* Registration fee for each trip.

When considering a travel club, just as in any other purchase, one would be wise to remember, "a bargain is not really a bargain unless you can use it."

CHAPTER 16

HIDDEN CITY DISCOUNTS

Airlines and travel agents don't like to mention the hidden city discount. It's not a discount you'll find advertised, rather a quirk produced by competition in a deregulated environment. Here's how it works: airlines competing on a route will lower their prices between two major cities so it's cheaper to fly, for example, between New York and Dallas than it is to fly from New York to St. Louis. In this example, if your destination was really St. Louis, you could buy a ticket from New York to Dallas on a flight that stops enroute in St. Louis. When you arrive in St. Louis, you get off.

The hidden city discount doesn't work for every destination, but there are enough cities where it works to make this trick worthwhile to the business traveler. Airlines frown on travel agents who knowingly sell the hidden city route to their clients. So much so that an agency might have their appointments revoked if it were discovered that they were advising clients to use this technique.

Most travel agents know about hidden city pairings, but really don't want to be put in the position of recommending this trick to their customers. The smart traveler can use an OAG and locate routes where this kind of ticketing will work. Then all one has to do is tell his travel agent which airline and flight he wants to take.

The key to locating the hidden city routings is to look for the city pairs involved in heavy competition among the airlines. If you regularly travel to a city somewhere between the city pairs involved in fare wars, then you may be in luck. For example, the following routes are usually involved in fare wars:

Los Angeles to — Chicago, Dallas, Denver, New York, Newark
San Francisco to — Chicago, Dallas, Denver, New York, Newark

Dallas to — New York, Chicago, Denver, Los Angeles, San Francisco

New York/Newark to — Los Angeles, San Francisco, Dallas, Atlanta, Miami, Chicago, Denver

Denver to — Los Angeles, San Francisco, Dallas, Houston, New York, Chicago

Chicago to — Los Angeles, San Francisco, Miami, Atlanta, New York, Washington

If your destination is a city between the above pairs, check the OAG carefully to locate a direct flight that makes a stop at your true destination.

The business traveler that isn't able to plan his trips far enough in advance, or with enough certainty to take advantage of advance purchase discount fares can use the hidden city advantage to lower the cost of at least half of the round trip flight. It would be unusual to find a destination where the hidden city technique would work in both directions. For example, if a traveler's real destination was St. Louis, and he was departing on a New York to Dallas flight with a stop in St. Louis, the hidden city routing would result in a savings on the New York to St. Louis segment, but not on the return portion, St. Louis to New York.

PRECAUTIONS

The airlines won't allow you to check your baggage to the hidden city; it can only be checked to the final destination on your ticket. So you'll have to travel with carry-on luggage, but since this trick is used mainly by businessmen on short trips, this seldom presents a problem.

If you find that the hidden city trick works on routes you normally travel, do your travel agent a favor: don't tell him what you're doing when you buy your airline tickets! If you don't mention the hidden city, chances are your travel agent won't either. If you purchase your tickets at the airport, you may invite the questions of an inquisitive airline reservationist, wondering why you don't want to purchase a round trip. Some travelers have been known in this situation to purchase the return segment for a fictitious person. When using the hidden city trick, most smart travelers use good judgment.

CHAPTER 17

MAJOR U.S. AND INT'L AIRPORTS

Notes on Convenience, Duty-Free Shopping and Transportation to City

Atlanta, GA — The new Hartsfield Atlanta International Airport is one of the largest and most modern in the U.S. Multi-terminals are connected by an underground tram. Duty free shop and currency exchange available. Online connections are easy, offline and international connections will take some time. Transportation to the city is by bus, taxi, or coach: allow approximately 20 to 30 minutes.

Baltimore/Washington — B.W.I. is a modern international airport, but connections to offline and international flights can require quite a bit of walking. Baltimore/Washington International is not usually crowded, and traffic seems to flow well. World Airways uses this airport for inexpensive flights to Europe. Currency exchange and duty free shops are available. Transportation to the city is by coach, bus, and taxi, taking approximately 25 to 60 minutes to Baltimore; 55 minutes to Washington.

Boston, MA — Logan International is a nice alternative to JFK airport for international flights because it's less crowded and more compact, so a bit easier to make connections. Currency exchange and duty free shops are available. Transportation to the city is by train (12 min.), coach or taxi; allow 15 minutes.

Chicago, IL — O'Hare airport is one of the busiest airports in the world. It is a major "hub" for connecting flights on American and United Airlines. When the new international terminal is completed, it will be one of the most modern in the U.S. Currency exchange is available, but duty free shopping is very limited at the present time. Transportation to the city is available by express train, coach, bus, and taxi, taking approximately 45 minutes.

Dallas/Ft. Worth, TX — This airport lives up to the Texas image —it's big and spread out! This is American Airlines' main "hub" and if you're connecting to another flight you should allow plenty of time, especially if you're making an offline connection. There's a tram system to take passengers between the different airline terminals and it also makes a stop at the airport hotel (good selection of restaurants and bars there). Currency exchange is available, but presently no duty-free shop. Transportation to the city is by coach or taxi; allow approximately 25 to 30 minutes.

Denver, CO — Stapleton International airport continues to be expanded, and additional construction will probably continue until a new airport is built. Plan on air traffic control delays and allow plenty of time for online and offline connections. Stapleton has grown to the point that a long walk is required to get between concourses. Expect to be approached by numerous groups requesting donations to varying causes. The ice cream shop between concourse "C" and "D" is great! The airport also has some unique Western shops. Currency exchange is available at insurance vendors, but no duty-free shopping. Transportation to the city is by coach, bus, and taxi, taking approximately 15 to 20 minutes. Limos are also available to the ski resorts.

Detroit MI — The Detroit airport is spread out, so plan to do a lot of walking for offline connections. International charter flights leave from the north terminal. Transportation to the city is by coach or taxi; allow approximately 40 minutes.

Houston, TX — The airport is spread out in a "U" shape with connecting underground train service between the terminals. Allow plenty of time for making offline connections. Online connections are convenient. Duty-free shopping and currency exchange are available. Transportation to the city is by coach, bus, or taxi, taking approximately 30 to 45 minutes.

Honolulu, HI — If you're arriving here and connecting to an inter-island flight, try to have your luggage checked through to your final destination. The Aloha and Hawaiian airlines terminal is a long walk from the main international arrivals terminal. Luggage for passengers departing for the U.S. must be checked by the plant inspection department; allow enough time! Currency exchange and duty-free shopping are available. Transportation to the city is by bus, coach, and taxi, taking approximately 25 to 35 minutes.

Kansas City, MO — Mid-Continent airport's design is unique with several semi-circular buildings housing different airlines' departure gates. No long walks down concourses and no apparent main terminal building. There's an inter-terminal tram to connect all the different terminals. Currency exchange is available, but no duty-free shops. World Airways and TWA have flights to Europe from Kansas City. Transportation to the city is by taxi (expensive), or coach; allow approximately 30 minutes since the airport is 17 miles from downtown.

Los Angeles, CA — Los Angeles International Airport is a traffic nightmare. Allow lots and lots of time to get around the airport's "U" shaped interior traffic flow. Improvements have been completed recently, and traffic flows better than before, but traffic jams have not been eliminated. Even using the inter-terminal bus you should still allow plenty of time for offline and international flight transfers. If the traffic looks bad, when you need to make offline connections, consider walking to your connecting airline's departure terminal instead of riding the free bus. Currency exchange and duty-free shopping are available. Transportation to the city is by coach, bus, and taxi. Travel time depends entirely on traffic and destination in Los Angeles.

Miami, FL — The international terminal is well-designed and even has a McDonald's restaurant. Connections to domestic airlines require quite a walk. Miami International has more service to South America, Central America, and the Caribbean than any other airport. Flights to Europe are rather limited. 24-hour currency exchange and large duty-free shops are available. Transportation to city via coach, taxi, and bus, taking approximately 25 to 30 minutes. Metrorail system from downtown to South Miami may be extended to the airport in the future.

Minneapolis, MN — The Minneapolis/St. Paul International airport is the main "hub" for Northwest Orient airlines. Most online connections are easy to make. Currency exchange is available, but no duty-free shop. Transportation to the city is by coach or taxi, taking approximately 25 to 30 minutes.

Newark, NJ — Home of PeoplExpress, Newark International has grown more popular for travelers seeking an alternative to JFK or LaGuardia airports. The old terminal building is used by PeoplExpress and a new terminal is used by all other airlines. I'm told that the PeoplExpress terminal is *very* crowded, but this isn't the case with the new terminal. Overall, it's a better alternative than JFK. A free inter-terminal bus connects the terminal buildings. Currency exchange is available and there is a duty-free shop. Transportation to the city is by coach, express bus, train or taxi; allow approximately 30 minutes.

New Orleans, LA — The main terminal building has been remodeled and remodeling of the concourses is in process. Some distinctly Southern dishes and fresh seafood are available at restaurants. Moisant Field is a major airport for flights to and from Central America. Duty-free shopping is available. Transportation to the city is by coach, bus, and taxi, taking approximately 25 to 40 minutes.

New York, JFK — One of the busiest and most spread out airports in the world. Brace yourself for crowds, confusion, and an exciting ride on the inter-terminal bus system! If you have a choice, avoid JFK for anything other than online connections. Transportation between international and domestic flights can seem to take hours if the airport is jammed with traffic (which is a frequent occurrence). Prices at airport shops and restaurants are high, and service is slow. Because of the volume of air traffic handled by JFK, delays are frequent, leaving or arriving. This airport is not the place to try to make a close connection. Currency exchange and duty-free shops are available. Transportation to the city is by bus, coach, taxi, and subway train; allow 45 to 60 minutes to downtown Manhattan. The JFK Express is one of the easier ways to get downtown when the traffic is heavy. Board the bus in front of the terminal, and it takes you to the subway station. Armed police ride the subway train!

Philadelphia, PA — Philadelphia International is another good alternative to JFK for flights to Europe. Although the airport has spread out, it's easier to make connections to other flights here. Currency exchange and duty-free shopping are available. Transportation to the city is by coach, bus, or taxi; allow approximately 30 to 40 minutes.

Portland, OR — Portland International is less crowded than many large airports, but offline connections still involve quite a bit of walking. Traffic flows well into and out of the airport. Currency exchange is available, but no duty-free shopping. Transportation to the city is by bus, coach, and taxi, allow approximately 20 to 30 minutes.

San Francisco, CA — San Francisco International airport has a great variety of restaurants and specialized food shops and one of the best bookstores of any U.S. airport. The layout is in a "C" shape with an inter-terminal bus to get you from the international terminal to the different domestic airlines departure gates. Currency exchange and duty-free shopping are available. Transportation to the city by taxi is expensive (approximately $20), but coach, and bus transportation is available for much less. Allow 35 to 40 minutes.

Seattle, WA — SeaTac airport is one of the more modern domestic/international airports on the West Coast. A system of underground trains connect passengers to different terminals. Access to airplanes from the underground train system involves a series of escalators. Currency exchange and duty-free shopping are available. Transportation to the city is by coach, bus, or taxi; allow approximately 25 to 45 minutes.

Tampa, FL — Tampa has one of the best designed airports in the U.S. Passengers are moved from a central terminal to individual airlines gates by an automatic tram. There is plenty of space and the baggage claim area is well **organized** for convenience to ground transportation. Passengers and pilots like this airport! The airport hotel is comfortable and well-soundproofed. A good variety of dining and shopping facilities is available. Currency exchange and duty-free shopping are available. Transportation to the city is by taxi; allow approximately 10 to 15 minutes.

Washington Dulles — This airport is an unloved stepchild to Baltimore/Washington International & Washington National airport. It's not attractive for domestic passengers bound for Washington D.C. because of its 27-mile distance from the Capitol. Transportation to airplanes from the main terminal is via mobile lounges. United Airlines and Presidential Airlines flights depart from gates that are reached without having to board a mobile lounge. Currency exchange and duty-free shops are available. Transportation to the city is by taxi (over $25.00) or coach; allow approximately 50 minutes.

CHAPTER 18

DUTY-FREE SHOPPING

Most people rate shopping high on their list of enjoyable activities when taking a trip abroad, whether to a neighboring country such as Canada or Mexico, or to Europe or the Far East. But travelers don't have to wait until they reach their destination to get bargain prices on certain luxury goods.

Duty-free shops give travelers the opportunity to save money on liquor, cigarettes, cigars, perfume, and other select luxury items when leaving or before returning to the U.S. Items sold at duty-free shops are being exported from the country so they cost less because the sales price does not include import duties and local taxes (VAT in Europe). (See appendix J for a listing of airports that have duty-free shops.)

You'll find duty-free shopping available at U.S. and foreign international airports, also aboard scheduled and charter airlines' international flights, although the inflight selection is generally much more limited than in airport shops.

Prices at duty-free shops vary greatly depending on the item(s) purchased and the country in which they're purchased. Certain U.S. made items are less expensive in U.S. duty-free stores than in foreign or inflight duty-free shops, for example, American cigarettes. Other items should always be purchased when departing the U.S. instead of waiting to purchase them at a foreign duty-free store before returning home. For example, Scotch whiskey is usually less expensive when purchased at U.S. duty-free prices, surprisingly, even when compared to prices at duty-free shops in London. But as a general rule, don't purchase items at a U.S. duty-free store that are manufactured in the country you're going to visit. Buying tequila at a duty-free store before a trip to Mexico doesn't make sense, neither does buying rum before a trip to the Caribbean, or French perfume before a trip to Paris. The only "catch" is that articles you purchase at U.S. duty-free shops *and bring back* with you into the U.S. cannot be included in your exemption and are dutiable!

The U.S. Customs Service sets a limit on the dollar value of items that can be brought back to the U.S. before you will be charged duty and Federal tax. If you've been out of the U.S. for 48 hours or more, you are exempt from duty and federal tax on the first $400.00 worth of goods obtained abroad. This exemption is reduced to only $25.00 if you're out of the U.S. for less than 48 hours, or have claimed the $400.00 exemption within the preceeding 30 days. You'll be given a Customs Declaration on board the plane to complete and turn in to the Customs officer when you re-enter the U.S. If you exceed the limits, you must pay duty, internal revenue tax and possibly state tax. Some people find it's still cheaper to purchase certain brands of liquor and luxury items at duty-free prices and pay the duty. But beware, there are some states that don't allow you to import more liquor even by paying the extra tax.

The next $1000.00 over the exemption amount is dutiable at a flat 10 percent rate. Each family member is allowed the exemption(s) above with the exception that children are not allowed to bring back alcoholic beverages.

Customs assumes that all foreign-made items you bring back into the U.S. were purchased abroad. Smart travelers arrive at their U.S. departure airport in time to take a list of their foreign-made cameras, watches, radios, tape recorders, etc., *with their serial numbers*, to the Customs office for registration *before* leaving. Once the serial numbers are registered with Customs, you don't have to worry about registering them again if you take another trip abroad. If you don't have time to register your foreign-made items, it would be prudent to take some proof with you to show that you purchased the items in the U.S. Acceptable proof can be a receipt, bill-of-sale, insurance policy, or jeweler's appraisal.

Special exemptions are available to travelers returning to the U.S. from the U.S. Virgin Islands (St. Thomas & St. Croix), Guam and American Somoa. From these destinations the exemption is increased to $800.00 and you're allowed five liters of liquor per adult instead of just one liter. Also, the next $1000.00 worth of goods purchased in these islands can br brought into the U.S. at a 5 percent flat rate of duty. The same 30-day time limit still applies.

Probably the most frequently purchased items in duty-free shops are liquor and perfume. A survey in January, 1985, by the Bureau Europeen des Unions de Consommateurs revealed that while airport duty-free shops were less expensive than shops in the neighboring city, the savings varied quite dramatically. In some cases, airport prices were as much as 55 percent lower than city prices, in other cities the price advantage was only 7 percent to 8 percent. The duty-free shop at the Amsterdam airport offered the greatest savings on liquor while Athens had the best prices for perfume.

Before you travel abroad, it's a good idea to check prices at local discount stores on items you plan to purchase abroad. You may be surprised to find that some cameras, radios, and watches can be purchased locally for the same price or even less than at duty-free stores.

The U.S. Customs Service has a brochure available that answers most questions first-time travelers may have about Customs regulations. You can request one by writing to: U.S. Customs, P.O. Box 7407, Washington, DC 20044, or phone (202) 566-8195.

When purchasing foreign-made goods abroad that may require servicing or repairs in the future, remember this basic rule: only buy a foreign-made product that is sold and serviced in the U.S., if there's a chance it might break or require adjustment during its normal useful life.

In many European countries, you can apply for a refund of Value Added Tax (VAT) on purchases made in regular shops: be sure to save all your receipts. Although it's a bit of a hassle, here's what you have to do: first make sure the store participates in the VAT rebate scheme; complete the form and take it, *with your purchase*, to the customs department at the airport when you are leaving the country. The customs officer signs the form and then sends a copy of it back to the shop. The shopkeeper then mails you a check for the VAT you paid. Obviously, this is a complicated procedure and makes it necessary for you to carry your purchases with you to present to the customs officer. Some merchants aren't too fond of all the paperwork required either, so it might be a good idea to ask first before you decide to make an expensive purchase. Other countries and cities are duty-free ports where no duty or tax are levied on items entering or leaving the country.

The U.S. Government has devised a system that exempts from duty many goods bought in certain developing countries. The Generalized System of Preferences (GSP) will allow you to exceed the $400 exemption without paying the flat-rate duty. Countries that participate include the Bahamas, Barbados, Dominican Republic, and Peru. Request the *GSP and the Traveler* pamphlet from the U.S. Customs Service for more information.

Some communist countries, Bulgaria, Romania, and Czechoslovakia, offer reduced prices for goods produced in their country if you pay in foreign currency at state-run stores.

My wife and I have traveled extensively in Europe, the Caribbean, Middle East, and Far East as flight crew members. In our experience the most fascinating duty-free store of all is located in Ireland's Shannon airport. It's so large that it resembles a department store. Listed below are some of the items we found to be especially good buys in local and/or duty-free shops in cities we visited:

Hong Kong — Cameras, radios, custom-made clothes, precious gems, electronics.

Dubai, U.A.E. — Gold jewelry (go to the gold market in town).

U.S. Virgin Is. — Rum, exotic liquors, perfume, crystal.

Athens, Greece — Perfume, liquor.

Amsterdam, Holland — Liquor

London — China, antiques, custom tailored suits, (don't miss Harrod's department store — you can buy *anything* there!)

Istanbul, Turkey — Alabaster, fur coats, suede & leather clothes.

Moscow — Fur coats, caviar, vodka.

Curacao, D.W.I. — Watches, jewelry, perfume, crystal, china.

Mexico — Locally produced liquor, Onyx chess and backgammon sets, leather goods, silver.

Spain — Leather goods, classical guitars, antiques, Lladero figurines.

Mallorca (Baleric Is.) — Cultured pearls

Ireland — Shannon's duty-free store for linen, wool sweaters, crystal, china, electronics

Singapore — Watches, radios, cameras, jade, silk, custom-made clothing, precious and semi-precious stones

Gibraltar — Best prices in Europe for cameras, liquor, perfume, embroidered lace tablecloths, watches, and electronics

Karachi — Onyx and silver

Tenerife — gold, watches, furs, liquor, leather goods

Rome — wine (Chianti), liquor, leather goods

Geneva — watches

Khartoum — Ivory

If you're traveling abroad for the first time, you may be shocked at the price and limited availability of American bourbon whiskey. Outside of the U.S., when one asks for whiskey, it usually is interpreted as meaning scotch whiskey. Bourbon drinkers would be wise to buy bourbon at a duty-free shop before leaving the U.S. American cigarettes are often difficult to find overseas and they're always more expensive. Smokers should take a supply of their favorite brand along on their trip. In some countries American cigarettes can be used to barter for gifts and souvenirs.

APPENDICES

MAJOR CITY THREE-LETTER IDENTIFICATION CODES

Find the destination city in the left-hand column and the three-letter city/airport code used by airlines in the right-hand column. The three-letter city/airport codes are used on luggage claim checks. Space has been left at the end of this appendix for you to add cities not included in this listing.

UNITED STATES, CANADA & MEXICO

City	Code	City	Code
Akron/Canton, OH	CAK	Dallas (Love Field), TX	DAL
Allentown, PA	ABE	Dayton, OH	DAY
Anchorage, AK	ANC	Denver, CO	DEN
Asheville, NC	AVL	Des Moines, IA	DSM
Atlanta, GA	ATL	Detroit (Wayne Co.), MI	DTW
Baltimore, MD	BWI	El Paso, TX	ELP
Bangor, ME	BGR	Fairbanks, AK	FAI
Bermuda, Atlantic Ocean	BDA	Ft. Lauderdale, FL	FLL
Boise, ID	BOI	Ft. Myers, FL	FMY
Boston, MA	BOS	Ft. Meyers (Regional), FL	RSW
Buffalo, NY	BUF	Ft. Wayne, IN	FWA
Calgary, Can.	YYC	Fresno, CA	FAT
Cancun, Mexico	CUN	Grand Rapids, MI	GRR
Charlotte, NC	CLT	Harrisburg, PA	MDT
Chicago (Midway), IL	MDW	Hartford/Springfield,	
Chicago (O'Hare), IL	ORD	CT	BDL
Cincinnati, OH	CVG	Hilo, Hawaii, HI	ITO
Cleveland, OH	CLE	Honolulu, Oahu, HI	HNL
Columbia, SC	CAE	Hot Springs, AR	HOT
Columbus, OH	CMH	Houston (Intrcont'l), TX	IAH
Corpus, Christi, TX	CRP	Houston, TX	HOU
Cozumel, Mexico	DFW	Ithaca, NY	ITH
Dallas/Ft. Worth, TX	DFW	Jackson, MS	JAN

Jacksonville, FL	JAX	Omaha, NB	OMA
Juneau, AK	JNU	Orange Co. (Santa Ana),	
Kansas City (Int'l), MO	MCI	CA	SNA
Kansas City, MO	MKC	Orlando, FL	MCO
Kauai, HI	LIH	Palm Springs, CA	PSP
Ketchikan, AK	KTN	Philadelphia, PA	PHL
Key West, FL	EYW	Phoenix, AZ	PHX
Knoxville, TN	TYS	Pittsburgh, PA	PIT
Kona, Hawaii, HI	KOA	Portland, ME	PWM
Lansing, MI	LAN	Portland, OR	PDX
Las Vegas, NV	LAS	Raleigh/Durham, NC	RDU
Little Rock, AR	LIT	Reno, NV	RNO
Lincoln, NB	LNK	Richmond, VA	RIC
Long Beach, CA	LGB	Rochester, NY	ROC
Los Angeles, CA	LAX	Sacramento, CA	SMF
Louisville, KY	SDF	Saginaw, MI	MBS
Madison, WS	MSN	San Diego, CA	SAN
Maui (Kaanapali) HI	HKP	San Jose, CA	SJC
Maui (Kahului), HI	OGG	San Juan, PR	SJU
Mazatlan, Mexico	MZT	San Francisco, CA	SFO
Memphis, TN	MEM	Seattle/Tacoma, WA	SEA
Mexico City, Mexico	MEX	Spokane, WA	GEG
Miami, FL	MIA	Syracuse, NY	SYR
Milwaukee, WS	MKE	Tampa (Intl), FL	TPA
Minnespolis/St. Paul, MN	MSP	Tampa/St. Petersburgh,	
Missoula, MT	MSO	FL	PIE
Moline, IL	MLI	Terre Haute, IN	HUF
Montgomery, AL	MGM	Toledo, OH	TOL
Montreal (Mirabel), Can.	YMX	Tucson, AZ	TUS
Nashville, TN	BNA	Toronto, Can.	YYZ
Nassau, Bahama Is.	NAS	Tulsa, OK	TUL
New Haven, CT	HVN	Utica, NY	UCA
Newark, NJ	EWR	Vancouver B.C., Can.	YVR
Newport News, VA	PHF	Washington, DC (Nat'l)	DCA
New Orleans, LA	MSY	Washington, DC (Dulles)	IAD
New York (Kennedy), NY	JFK	West Palm Beach, FL	PBI
New York (LaGuardia),		White Plains, NY	HPN
NY	LGA	Wichita, KS	ICT
Oakland, CA	OAK	Wilmington, DE	ILG
Oklahoma City, OK	OKC	Winnipeg, Can.	YWG

CARIBBEAN, EUROPE, ASIA, AFRICA & THE FAR EAST

Abidjan, Ivory Coast	ABJ	Cap Haitien, Haiti	CAP
Addis Ababa, Ethiopia	ADD	Caracas, Venequela	CCS
Amman, Jordan	AMM	Casablanca, Morocco	CAS
Amsterdam, Netherlands	AMS	Christchurch, New	
Antigua, West Indies	ANU	Zealand	CHC
Antwerp, Belgium	ANR	Colombo, Sri Lanka	CMB
Aruba, Netherland		Copenhagen, Denmark	CPH
Antillies	AUA	Corfu, Greece	CFU
Asuncion, Paraguay	ASU	Curacao, Netherland	
Athens, Greece	ATH	Antillies	CUR
Auckland, New Zealand	AKL	Dakar, Senegal	DKR
Bahrain, Bahrain	BAH	Damascus, Syria	DAM
Banjul, Gambia	BJL	Dar Es Salaam, Tanzania	DAR
Bangkok, Thailand	BKK	Delhi, India	DEL
Barbados, West Indies	BGI	Dhahran, Saudi Arabia	DHA
Barcelona, Spain	BCN	Dubai, U.A. Emirates	DXB
Beijing, China	PEK	Dublin, Ireland	DUB
Belgrade, Yugoslavia	BEG	Dusseldorf, Germany	DUS
Belize City, Belize	BZE	Durban, South Africa	DUR
Bergen, Norway	BGO	Edinburgh, Scotland (U.K.)	EDI
Berlin, West Germany	BER	Fez, Morocco	FEZ
Bermuda	BDA	Florence, Italy	FLR
Bogota, Colombia	BOG	Fort de France,	
Bombay, India	BOM	Martinique	FDF
Bora Bora, French		Frankfurt, Germany	FRA
Polynesia	BOB	Funchal, Maderia	
Brussels, Belgium	BRU	(Portugese)	FNC
Bucharest, Romania	BUH	Geneva, Switzerland	GVA
Bucharest (Baneasa)		Georgetown, Guyana	GEO
Romania	BBU	Gibraltar, Gibralter	GIB
Bucharest (Otopeni),		Glasgow, Scotland (U.K.)	GLA
Romania	OTP	Glasgow, (Prestwick),	
Budapest, Hungary	BUD	Scotland	PKI
Buenos Aires, Argentina	BUE	Grand Cayman, West	
Buenos Aires (Ezeiza),		Indies	GCM
Argentina	EZE	Grenada, Windward Is.	GND
Cairo, Egypt	CAI	Guatemala City,	
Calcutta, India	CCU	Guatemala	GUA
Capetown, South Africa	CPT	Guayaquil, Ecuador	GYE

Haifa, Israel	HFA	Madrid, Spain	MAD
Hamburg, Germany	HAM	Malacca, Malaysia	MKZ
Hanover, Germany	HAJ	Malaga, Spain	AGP
Helsinki, Finland	HEL	Malta, Malta	MLA
Hong Kong, Hong Kong	HKG	Managua, Nicaragua	MGA
Ibiza, Spain	IBZ	Manchester, England	MAN
Islamabad/Rawalpindi,		Manila, Philippines	MNL
Pakistan	IBS	Marrakech, Morocco	RAK
Isle of Man, (U.K.)	IOM	Marseille, France	MRS
Istanbul, Turkey	IST	Mauritius, Maritius	MRU
Jakarta (Halim),		Melbourne, Australia	MEL
Indonesia	HLP	Montego Bay, Jamaica	MBJ
Jeddah, Saudi Arabia	JED	Montevideo, Uruguay	MVD
Jersey, Channel Is. (U.K.)	JER	Montserrat, West Indies	MNI
Johannesburg, South		Moscow (Sheremetye),	
Africa	JNB	U.S.S.R.	SVO
Kabul, Afghanistan	KBL	Munich, Germany	MUC
Karachi, Pakistan	KHI	Nairobi, Kenya	NBO
Kathmandu, Nepal	KTM	Nassau, Bahamas	NAS
Khartoum, Sudan	KRT	Naples, Italy	NAP
Kingston, Jamaica	KIN	Nice, France	NCE
Kuala Lumpur, Malaysia	KUL	Oslo, Norway	OSL
Kuwait, Kuwait	KWI	Pago Pago, Samoa	PPG
La Paz, Bolivia	LPB	Palma, Mallorca Is.	
Las Palmas, Canary Is.	LPA	(Spain)	PMT
Le Havre, France	LEH	Panama City, Panama	PAC
Lima, Peru	LIM	Papeete, French Polynesia	PPT
Lisbon, Portugal	LIS	Paramaribo (Z-en Hoop),	
London (Gatwick)		Surinam	RGO
England	LGW	Paris (DeGaulle), France	CDG
London (Heathrow),		Paris (Orly), France	ORY
England	LHR	Penang, Malaysia	PEN
London (Luton Intl),		Perth, Australia	PER
England	LTN	Pointe A Pitre,	
London (Stansted),		Guadeloupe	PTP
England	STN	Port Au Prince, Haiti	PAP
Luxembourg,		Port Moresby, Papua	
Luxembourg	LUX	New Guinea	OMP
Luxor, Egypt	LXR	Port of Spain, Trinidad &	
Lyon, France	LYS	Tobago	POS

Prague, Czechoslovakia	PRG	Tenerife, Canary Is.	TFS
Quito, Ecuador	UTO	Tokyo (Narita), Japan	NRT
Rangoon, Burma	RGN	Tokyo (Haneda), Japan	HND
Reykjavik, Iceland	REK	Tortola, British V.I.	EIS
Reykjavik-Keflavik,		Trieste, Italy	TRS
Iceland	KEF	Tunis, Tunisia	TUN
Rio De Janeiro, Brazil	RIO	Vienna, Austria	VIE
Riyadh, Saudi Arabia	RUH	Venice, Italy	VCE
Roatan, Honduras	RTB	Warsaw, Poland	WAW
Rome (Fiumicino), Italy	FCO	Zagreb, Yugoslavia	ZAG
St. Croix, U.S.V.I.	STX	Zurich, Switzerland	ZRH
St. Kitts, Leeward Is.	SKB		
St. Lucia, West Indies	SLU		
St. Maarten, Neth.			
Antillies	SXM		
St. Thomas, U.S.V.I.	STT		
St. Vincent, Windward is.	SVD		
San Jose, Costa Rica	SJO		
San Juan, Puerto Rico	SJU		
San Salvador, El Salvador	SAL		
Santiago, Chile	SCL		
Santo Domingo,			
Dominican Rep.	SDQ		
Sao Paulo, Brazil	SAO		
Sao Paulo (Congonhas)			
Brazil	CGH		
Seoul, Korea	SEL		
Shanghai, China	SHA		
Shannon, Ireland	SNN		
Singapore, Singapore	SIN		
Sofia, Bulgaria	SOF		
Stockholm, Sweden	STO		
Stockholm (Arlanda),			
Sweden	ARN		
Stuttgart, Germany	STR		
Suva, Fiji	SUV		
Sydney, Australia	SYD		
Taipei, Taiwan	TPE		
Tegucigalpa, Honduras	TGU		
Tel Aviv (Yafo), Israel	TLV		

AIRLINE TWO-LETTER CODES AND TOLL-FREE FREE PHONE NUMBERS

Following is a list of domestic and international airlines that have service to, or within the U.S. Each airline has a two-letter code. This code is used on airline tickets, in airlines' computer system and the OAG (Official Airline Guide).

Aer Lingus	EI	*
Aeromexico	AM	800 237-6639 (Ex. AK, HI)
American Airlines	AA	800 433-7300
America West	HP	800 247-5692 (Ex. AK)
Alaksa Airlines	AS	800 426-0333 (Ex. AK, AB, BC, SK)
Air Afrique	RK	*
Air Atlanta	CC	*
Air Cal	OC	800 424-7225 (Ex. AK, CA)
Air Canada	AC	800 422-6232 (Ex. AK)
Air France	AF	*
Air India	AI	*
Air Jamaica	JM	*
Air New Zealand	TE	*
Air Panama	OP	*
Alitalia	AZ	800 223-5730 (Ex. AK, NY)
Alia Royal Jordanian	RJ	800 223-0470 (Ex. AK, NY)
Aloha	AQ	*
Avianca	AV	800 327-9899 (Ex. AK)
Braniff	BN	800 272-6433 (Ex. AK)
British Airways	BA	800 847-4400 (Ex. AK, HI, NY)
British Caledonian	BR	800 231-0270 (Ex. AK, TX)
BWIA International	BW	*

Cathay Pacific	CX	*
Cayman Airways	KX	800 422-9626 (Ex. AK)
Continental	CO	800 525-0280 (Ex. AK, HI)
CP Air	CP	*
Delta	DL	*
Dominicana	DO	*
Eastern	EA	800 327-8376 (Ex. AK)
El Al	LY	*
Egyptair	MS	*
Finnair	AY	800 223-5700 (Ex. AK, NY)
Florida Express	ZO	800 327-8538 (Ex. AK, FL)
Frontier	FL	*
Garuda Indonesian	GA	*
Hawaiian	HA	800 367-5320 (Ex. AK, HI)
Iberia	IB	*
Icelandair	FI	800 223-5500 (Ex. AK, NY)
Japan Airlines	JL	800 525-3663 (Ex. AK)
Jet America	SI	*
Korean	KE	800 421-8200 (Ex. AK, CA)
Lufthansa	LH	800 645-3800 (Ex. AK, NY)
Mexicana	MX	800 531-7921 (Ex. AK)
Mid Pacific	HO	*
Midway	ML	*
Midwest Express	YX	800 452-2002 (Ex. AK, WI)
New York Air	NY	
Northwest Orient	NW	*
Olympic	OA	*
Ozark	OZ	*
Pacific Western	PW	*
Pakistan International	PK	*
Pan American	PA	*
PeoplExpress	PE	*
Phillipine Airlines	PR	*
Piedmont	PI	*
Presidential	XV	*
PSA	PS	*
Quantas	QF	*
Republic	RC	*
Royal Air Moroc	AT	*
Sabena	SN	*

SAS	SK	*
Saudia	SV	*
Singapore	SQ	*
South African Airways	SA	*
Southwest	WN	*
Swissair	SR	*
TAP Portugese	TP	*
Thai Airways	TG	*
Tower Air	FF	*
TWA	TW	*
United	UA	*
U.S.Air	AL	*
UTA	UT	*
Varig	RG	*
Virgin Atlantic	VS	*
Western	WA	*
World Airways	WO	*

* No Nationwide 800 Number. Phone toll-free information for number.

DECIPHERING AIRLINE TERMINOLOGY

Airlines have been confusing the consumer for years with their exclusive language. Some of the terms used by airlines are straightforward, others have a hidden meaning. Some nasty surprises can be avoided by learning airline lingo.

To add to the confusion, a recent trend in the airline industry has been the pseudo-merging of air taxis and commuter airlines into the major airlines' flight schedules and computer system. This practice is known in the airline industry as "code-sharing."For example, there are quite a few commuter airlines flying under the name, American Eagle. These flights are shown in airline computer systems as American Airlines' flights. The only way to differentiate between them and American is the flight numbers assigned to the commuter airlines. Not all of this is bad — it enables one to gain mileage credits for flying from outlying airports to connect with the major airline. Also, the commuter schedule more than likely has been aligned to connect with the sponsoring major airline. The problem occurs when passengers are expecting to board a large airplane and find a small propeller driven airplane waiting to take them to their connecting flight.

The airport codes for each city that a flight landed at before reaching its final destination used to be printed in the airlines' flight schedules. Many airlines have eliminated this practice. This can cause problems when the connection is out of the way. A passenger choosing to fly between Los Angeles and Florida on PeoplExpress for example might find that the trip takes over 16 hours after connecting in Newark, NJ to the Florida flight, yet the passenger might be told by the airline that he's booked on a direct flight (see below).

GLOSSARY OF AIRLINE TERMINOLOGY

Non-Stop — A flight that goes directly between two points without stopping.

Direct Flight — A flight that makes one or more stops before reaching its final destination. Although you'll be making stops, you remain on the same airplane.

On-Line Connection — A flight totally on one airline although you will have to change airplanes somewhere before reaching your final destination.

Off-Line Connection — A flight in which you will have to change airlines at some point before reaching your final destination.

Illegal Connection — A connecting time between two flights that does not meet the minimum time requirements for the airport at which the passenger must change airplanes.

Open Jaw — A roundtrip ticket that has an open segment. For example, a routing from Los Angeles to New York then surface transportation to Boston then back to Los Angeles.

Open Return — A roundtrip ticket with no reservations for the return flight. The passenger should call the airlines and make the return reservation when the travel date is determined.

Off-Peak — A flight that departs very early or very late in the day. Generally a flight that is not popular with businessmen.

Waitlisted — Means that your name has been placed on a list for an oversold flight. If the airline receives enough cancellations, you will get a reserved seat if you're on the Waitlist.

Check-In — This means to show your airline ticket to the airline ticket agent or passenger agent either at the ticket counter or the departure gate. Even with advance seat selection and boarding passes issued by a travel agent, check-in is still required.

Reconfirm — Means to phone the airline before departure to confirm that you are still planning to use your ticket on your reserved flight. Some airlines will cancel your reservations if your return reservations are not reconfirmed within a set time limit (usually 24 hours) before departure.

Widebody Aircraft — Refers to a B-747, DC-10, L-1011, B-767, or AIRBUS.

Narrowbody Aircraft — Any of the earlier generation airliners such as the DC-8, B-707, B-727, B-737, DC-9, and the new B-757.

COMPARISON OF FREQUENT FLYER PROGRAMS

Airline	# Miles for Free Flight	Other Airlines	Hotels	Sign-up mi. credit	Car Rental
United	50,000	7 (c)	3	3,000	Hertz Budget
Republic	20,000	2 (c)	None	1,000	National Hertz
U.S. Air	20,000	(c)	None	1,000	None
Ozark	20,000		3	None	Budget Hertz
Midway	(3) 5		1	None	Budget
Eastern	40,000	5 (e) (c)	3	5,000	Dollar Hertz General
N.W. Orient	40,000	2 (c)	6	None	Thrifty National
Delta	40,000	2 (c)	2	5,000	Alamo National
Piedmont	30,000	1 (c)	1	2,500	Hertz
TWA	50,000	3 (c)	2	3,000	Hertz
American	50,000	4 (c)	3	3,000	Avis
Pan Am ($)	30,000 (m)	1	2	None	Hertz
Western	30,000	1 (c)	2	1,000	Budget Hertz
Continental ($)	35,000	3 (c)	1	5,000	Thrifty National
Frontier	20,000	None	None	None	Avis

(3) Mileage is not monitored, round-trips used to qualify.
(c) Some commuter airline included.
(e) Mileage credit on TWA (domestic), CP AIR, Aer Lingus (to Ireland) British Caledonian (to Britain), SAS (to Scandinavia) or TWA (to Europe).
($) A non-refundable $25.00 fee is charged for enrollment.
(m) Must travel Monday through Thursday.

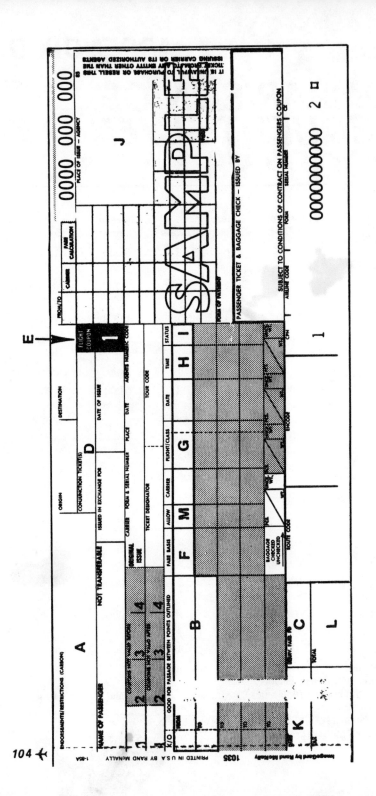

Note: Unless "OK" is in the status box (I), your reservation is *not* confirmed.

104

THE AIRLINE TICKET

Note the location of the various ticket codes in the illustration on page 104.

A. Time or date restrictions.

B. Departure — destination airports.

C. Local currency equivalent if ticket bought with foreign currency.

D. If another ticket had to be issued to cover the trip itinerary, then the reference number for additional tickets is noted here.

E. Each individual ticket coupon is numbered and can only be used for one flight.

F. Fare basis tells which set of rules governed the purchase price for your ticket.

G. Flight number and class.

H. Departure time (local).

I. Unless "OK" is in this box, your reservation is *not* confirmed.

J. This box must have either a travel agency stamp or airline validation.

K. Base Fare (excluding tax).

L. Total price paid for ticket.

M. Either "X" (stopover permitted), or "0" (no stopover allowed) will be in this space.

FARE CODES AND WHAT THEY MEAN

The airlines are free to change the restrictions on the different fares as free market competition dictates. While the fare codes listed below were accurate at the time of writing, changes are possible without any advance notice to the public.

PRIMARY FARE CODES:

Prime codes, may appear in the ticket's Fare Basis box alone or precede seasonal and/or fare type codes.

A — First Class Discounted

B — Coach Economy Discounted

C — Business Class

D — Business Class Discounted

F — First Class

H — Coach Economy Discounted

J — Business Class Premium

K — Thrift

L — Thrift Discounted

M — Coach Economy Discounted

P — First Class Premium

Q — Coach Economy Discounted

R — Supersonic

S — Standard Class

T — Coach Economy Discounted

U — No Reservation Service (Used on Standby Tickets)

SEASONAL CODES:

Will be indicated if applicable after the primary fare code.

H — Highest level of a fare having more than one seasonal level
O — 2nd level of a fare having more than two seasonal levels
J — 3rd level of a fare having more than three seasonal levels
Z — 4th level of a fare having more than four seasonal levels
T — 5th level of a fare having more than five seasonal levels
L — Lowest level of a fare having more than one seasonal level

Some fares are based on the season; these codes are arranged from highest level to lowest level. For example, if the fare is the lowest available in coach, the fare basis box of the ticket might indicate "YL."

PART OF WEEK CODE:

W = Weekend — applies to fares valid for weekend travel only
X = Weekday — applies to fares valid for weekday travel only

PART OF DAY CODE:

N = Night
Day flights do not have a code letter.

SURCHARGE CODE:

These codes are sometimes followed by one to three numbers to indicate the maximum validity of the ticket in days or one digit followed by "M" to indicate the maximum validity of the ticket in months.

AB = Advance Purchase
AF = Area Fare
AP = Advance Purchase
B = Budget
E = Excursion
IP = Instant Purchase
OX = One Way Excursion
RW = Round the World
S = Super Saver
U = No Advance Reservation Permitted
U = Standby Fare — Used following a prime code

QUALIFYING CODES:

Suffixes used in the fare basis box.

E = Excursion fares
EX = Excursion Fare

DISCOUNT DESIGNATOR:

D = A discounted fare if not already indicated by the primary fare code.

SAMPLE DISCOUNT FARE CODES
AND WHAT THEY MEAN

APEX = Advance Purchase Excursion Fare
BE7D = Coach Economy 7-day advance purchase, discounted
YU = Coach Standby fare
YHAP3M = Coach 3 month advance purchase fare
YD14 = 14 day advance purchase discounted coach
YLE6M = Lowest 6-month advance purchase excursion fare

SEAT NUMBERING

Most airlines use a standardized seat-numbering protocol. Seat rows are numbered from the front of the airplane to the back with the first row being numbered "1". Seats in each row are identified by letters of the alphabet starting with the letter "A" for the far left seat in each row viewed from the rear of the aircraft. Narrow body airplanes usually have six or fewer seats in each row. Widebody airplanes can have up to eleven. Illustrated on pages 110-113 are the seat designations used by the airlines. The passenger agent at the departure gate will either write your seat assignment on your ticket envelope or give you a boarding pass with this information on it. When you board the airplane, the seat row numbers are usually located on the overhead luggage bins or on the armrest of the aisle seats.

NARROWBODY AIRPLANE COACH-CLASS SEATING

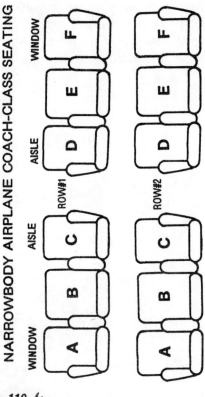

WINDOW   AISLE   AISLE   WINDOW

ROW#1

ROW#2

NARROWBODY AIRPLANE FIRST-CLASS SECTION

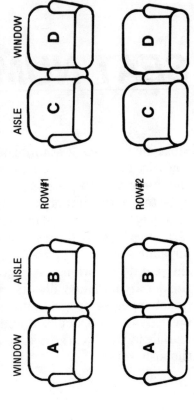

WINDOW   AISLE   AISLE   WINDOW

ROW#1

ROW#2

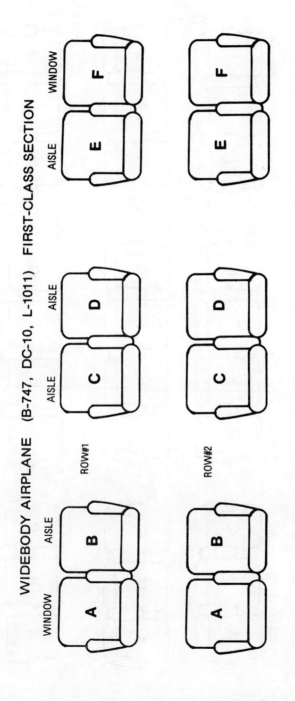

WIDEBODY AIRPLANE (B-747, DC-10, L-1011) FIRST-CLASS SECTION

WIDEBODY AIRPLANE (B-747, some DC-10) COACH-CLASS SEATING

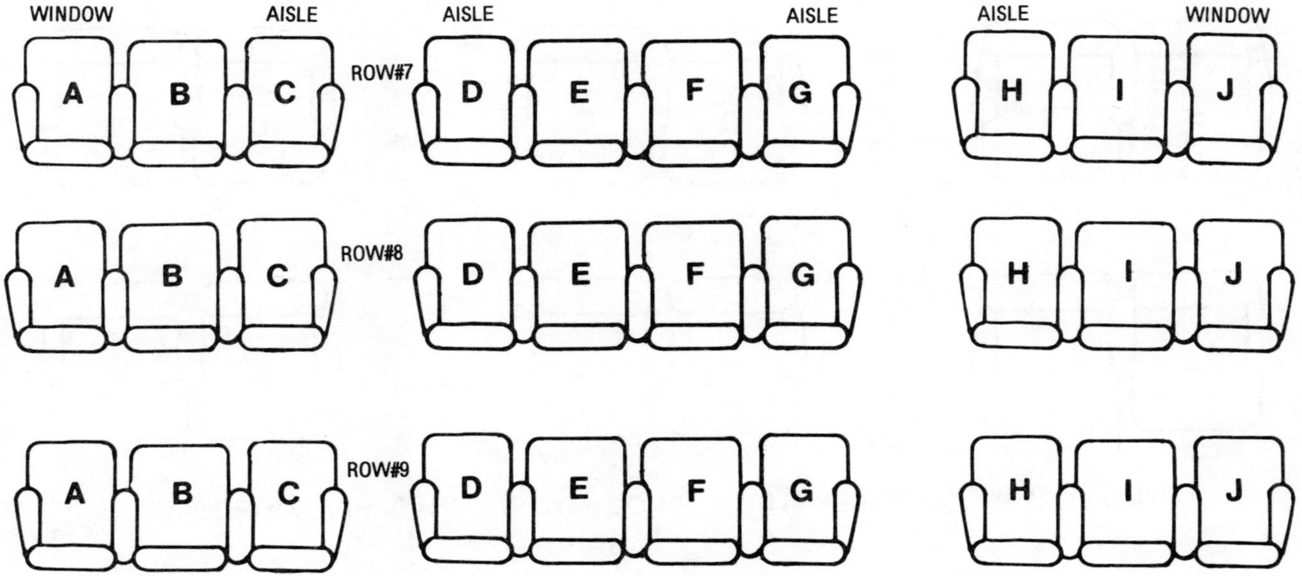

WINDOW
AISLE
AISLE
AISLE
AISLE
WINDOW
ROW#7
A B C D E F G H I J
ROW#8
A B C D E F G H I J
ROW#9
A B C D E F G H I J

WIDEBODY AIRCRAFT (most DC-10, L-1011, A-300) COACH CLASS SEATING

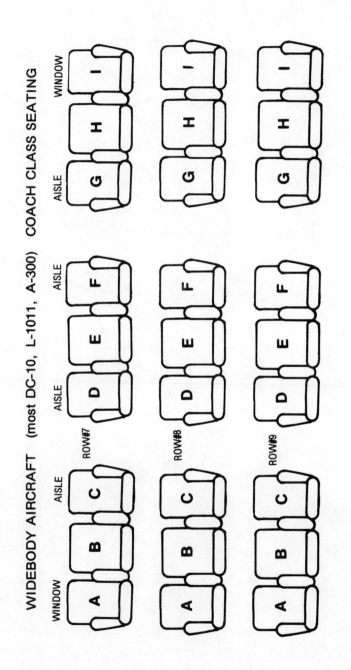

MINIMUM CHECK-IN TIMES

AIRLINE	MINIMUM TIME*
American	15 minutes
Continental	10 minutes
Delta	15 minutes
Eastern	15 minutes
Frontier	30 minutes
Piedmont	20 minutes
Republic	10 minutes
TWA	30 minutes
United	10 minutes
Western	30 minutes

* Minimum time before departure to check-in at the gate.

Airlines can cancel your reservation or reassign your seat if you don't meet their minimum check-in time requirements.

INTERNATIONAL BAGGAGE ALLOWANCE

Two methods are used to determine how much baggage passengers are allowed to carry free of charge. Each international airline can set their own limit using either the *Weight Method* or the *Piece Method*. For travel between points in the U.S./Canada and points outside the U.S./Canada, the *piece method* is generally the prevailing guideline used by the airlines.

The *weight method*, besides varying by airline, and class of service also varies by country. From Argentina, most airlines do not charge for baggage until a passenger exceeds a 33-pound limit; from Peru, the free allowance is 44 pounds. Exceptions to the general rule *weight-method* are listed in the OAG and travel agent's computer system. It would be a good idea to inquire about the free baggage allowance before departure.

WEIGHT METHOD

CLASS OF SERVICE	ALLOWANCE*
For Full-Fare Passengers:	
First/Business Class	66 lbs. (30 kg.)
Tourist/Coach/Economy/ Thrift	44 lbs. (20 kg.)
For Children:	
Paying 50% or more of full fare	Same as full-fare passengers
Paying 10% of adult fare	None
Infants carried free	None

**Checked and unchecked (carry-on).

PIECE METHOD

CLASS OF SERVICE	MAX PIECES		MAX WGT.*
	Checked	Carry-on	(Per bag)
First Business paying full-fare:	2	1 or more	
Economy/Executive Tourist/Coach Thrift/Other:	2	1 or more	70 lbs. (32 kg.)
Children paying 50% of adult fare:	2	1 or more	70 lbs. (32 kg.)
Children paying 10% of adult fare:	1	None	
Infants carried free:	None	None	

*Excludes carry-on.

TRAVEL REFERENCE SOURCES AND COMPUTER SERVICES/ DATABASES

FLIGHT SCHEDULES:

Official Airline Guide Electronic Edition — Lists the arrival and departure times for all airlines at all airports in the world. The information is updated weekly. Access is through CompuServe with additional fees for online time.

Travel Fax — A computer data base of travel related information on customs, currency, holiday information, weather, and other facts about foreign countries. It's available through CompuServe.

Airschedules — A computer data base of domestic and international flights. Includes fare types and additional information. This system will suggest possible flights after you enter your departure point and destination. Available to The Source subscribers.

CURRENCY EXCHANGE:

Currency Exchange Data Base — This computer data base provides currency exchange rate data for 59 currencies. It has the opening and closing rates as well as some historical data. Available with no subscription or minimum monthly service charge through the General Electric online service.

Currency — This computer data base, updated three times daily gives, the current exchange rate. Available through The Source.

TRAVEL REFERENCES:

The books/magazines/newsletters listed below are good sources of information about customs, accommodations, sightseeing, and other information you might find useful when planning a trip.

Airfare Discount Bulletin§
Consumer Reports Travel Letter°
Club Costa Magazine§
Fodor's Travel Guides
Frommer's Travel Guides
Pan Am Travel Guides
Mobil Travel Guides
Birnbaums Travel Guides
OAG Travel Planning Guides*
OAG*

* The OAG is also issued in handy pocket-size books. Editions that cover airline schedules for every part of the world are available: To order toll-free phone (800) 323-3537.

† Available from ADB Publishing, Riverside, CT.

‡ Available by subscription, back issues also available; write to: Consumer Reports Travel Letter, Box 5248, Boulder, CO 80322.

§ Only available to members of ADCI/Club Costa. For membership information, phone (800) 225-0381.

INTERNATIONAL AIRPORTS WITH DUTY-FREE SHOPS

CITY	CODE	Customs Assistance Local Telephone Number
Abidjan, Ivory Coast	ABJ	
Addis Ababa, Ethiopia	ADD	
Amsterdam, Netherlands	AMS	
Antigua, West Indies	ANU	
Aruba, Netherland Antillies	AUA	
Athens, Greece	ATH	
Auckland, New Zealand	AKL	
Bahrain, Bahrain	BAH	
Bangkok, Thailand	BKK	
Barbados, West Indies	BGI	
Belgrade, Yugoslavia	BEG	
Belize City, Belize	BZE	
Bergen, Norway	BGO	
Berlin, West Germany	BER	
Bermuda	BDA	
Bogota, Colombia	BOG	
Bombay, India	BOM	
Brussels, Belgium	BRU	513-3830
Bucharest, Romania	BUH	
Budapest, Hungary	BUD	
Cairo, Egypt	CAI	
Calcutta, India	CCU	
Caracas, Venezuela	CCS	
Christchurch, New Zealand	CHC	
Colombo, Sri Lanka	CMB	
Copenhagen, Denmark	CPH	

Curacao, Netherland Antillies	CUR	_____
Dakar, Senegal	DKR	_____
Damascus, Syria	DAM	_____
Dar Es Salaam, Tanzania	DAR	_____
Delhi, India	DEL	_____
Dubai, U.A. Emirates	DXB	_____
Dublin, Ireland	DUB	_____
Dusseldorf, Germany	DUS	_____
Frankfurt, Germany	FRA	_____
Geneva, Switzerland	GVA	_____
Georgetown, Guyana	GEO	_____
Gibraltar, Gibraltar	GIB	_____
Glasgow, Scotland (U.K.)	GLA	_____
Guatemala City Guatemala	GUA	_____
Guayaquil, Ecuador	GYE	_____
Hamburg, Germany	HAM	_____
Hanover, Germany	HAJ	_____
Helsinki, Finland	HEL	_____
Hong Kong, Hong Kong	HKG	283-010
Istanbul, Turkey	IST	_____
Jakarta (Halim), Indonesia	HLP	_____
Jersey, Channel Is. (U.K.)	JER	_____
Johannesburg, South Africa	JNB	_____
Karachi, Pakistan	KHI	_____
Kathmandu, Nepal	KTM	_____
Khartoum, Sudan	KRT	_____
Kingston, Jamaica	KIN	_____
Kuala Lumpur, Malaysia	KUL	_____
Lima, Peru	LIM	_____
Lisbon, Portugal	LIS	_____
London (Gatwick), England	LGW	499-1212
London (Heathrow), England	LHR	_____

City	Code	Phone
London (Luton Intl), England	LTN	_____
Luxembourg, Luxembourg	LUX	_____
Lyon, France	LYS	_____
Madrid, Spain	MAD	_____
Malta, Malta	MLA	_____
Managua, Nicaragua	MGA	_____
Manchester, England	MAN	_____
Manila, Philippines	MNL	_____
Marseille, France	MRS	_____
Melbourne, Australia	MEL	_____
Montevideo, Uruguay	MVD	_____
Moscow (Sheremetye), U.S.S.R.	SVO	_____
Munich, Germany	MUC	_____
Nairobi, Kenya	NRO	_____
Nice, France	NCE	_____
Oslo, Norway	OSL	_____
Panama City, Panama	PAC	_____
Papeete, French Polynesia	PPT	_____
Paramaribo (Z-en Hoop), Surinam	RGO	_____
Paris (DeGaulle), France	CDG	296-1201, ext. 2392
Paris (Orly), France	ORY	296-1201, ext. 2392
Penang, Malaysia	PEN	_____
Perth, Australia	PER	_____
Port Moresby, Papua New Guinea	OMP	_____
Port of Spain, Trinidad & Tobago	POS	_____
Prague, Czechoslovakia	PRG	_____
Quito, Ecuador	UTO	_____
Reykjavik, Iceland	REK	_____
Rome (Fiumicino), Italy	FCO	6/4674, ext. 475 or 533
St. Lucia, West Indies	SLU	_____
San Jose, Costa Rica	SJO	_____

San Juan, Puerto Rico	SJU	_____
San Salvador, El Salvador	SAL	_____
Santo Domingo, Dominican Rep.	SDQ	_____
Seoul, Korea	SEL	_____
Shannon, Ireland	SNN	_____
Singapore, Singapore	SIN	_____
Sofia, Bulgaria	SOF	_____
Stockholm, Sweden	STO	_____
Stuttgart, Germany	STR	_____
Sydney, Australia	SYD	_____
Taipei, Taiwan	TPE	_____
Tegucigalpa, Honduras	TGU	_____
Tel Aviv (Yafo), Israel	TLV	_____
Tokyo (Narita), Japan	NRT	583-7141, ext. 7205
Tokyo)Haneda), Japan	HND	583-7141, ext. 7205
Vienna, Austria	VIE	_____
Warsaw, Poland	WAW	_____
Zagreb, Yugoslavia	ZAG	_____
Zurich, Switzerland	ZRH	_____